COOKING
Made Easy

BRIMAR

The dairy products logo 🐮 is a Registered
Certification Mark of the Dairy Farmers of Canada.
The Registered Certification Mark was created to
guarantee and authenticate products which are
made exclusively with Canadian milk and meet
the standards of Agriculture Canada.

© 1996 Brimar Publishing Inc.
338 Saint Antoine St. East
Montreal, Canada H2Y 1A3
Tel. (514) 954-1441
Fax (514) 954-5086

Graphic Design: Zapp
Typesetting, Color Separation and Films: Caractéra
Photography: Rodrigo Gutierrez
Food Preparation/Stylist: Josée Robitaille
Assistant Stylist: Louis Hudon
Props courtesy of: Pier 1 Imports
                      Arthur Quentin
                      Stokes

Pictured on the front cover:
Turkey Breast Parmigiana (see page 124) and
Old-Fashioned Cheesecake (see page 166)

We gratefully acknowledge recipe contributions
from the Dairy Farmers of Ontario.

Please forward any requests, questions or
comments to:
Cooking Made Easy
SIMPLY DELICIOUS RECIPES
USING CANADIAN DAIRY PRODUCTS
1981 McGill College Avenue
Suite 1330
Montreal, Quebec
H3A 2X9

Canadian Cataloguing in Publication Data
   Cooking made easy: simply delicious recipes
   using Canadian dairy products
Issued also in French under title: Cuisine facile –
   Recettes simples et délicieuses avec les produits
   laitiers de chez nous

Includes index.
ISBN 2-89433-272-6
   1. Cookery (Dairy products).
TX759.C6614 1996   641.6'7   C96-900480-X

Printed in Canada

COOKING
Made Easy

Contents

COOKING
Made Easy

As a source of health and well-being, dairy products make up an important part of our daily diet. Rich in protein, vitamins and minerals, these tasty foods come in many different forms, making it easy for you to eat the two to four daily servings recommended by *Canada's Food Guide to Healthy Eating.*

Example of one serving of milk product:

1 cup (250 mL) of milk
50 g of firm cheese
¾ cup (175 g) of yogourt
¾ cup (175 g) of ice cream

But besides being healthy, versatile foods, dairy products are also quick and easy to prepare. Through this beautifully illustrated cookbook, Canadian dairy farmers are proud to present 150 simple and delicious recipes, all made with Canadian dairy products. From mouth-watering appetizers and soups to main dishes, flavourful vegetables and exquisite desserts, the kitchen-tested recipes contained in this volume will show you that dairy products are just as appropriate for elaborate meals as they are for simple snacks.

Try our helpful tips and interesting variations. Look for the tiny cow 🐄 to find out how to alternate cheeses to create a slightly different-tasting recipe that is just as nutritious and delicious. Remember, when you've got cheese, you've got choice.

From our kitchen to yours, we hope that you will enjoy these recipes and make your culinary experience a success, every time.

Canadian Dairy Products

Canada's dairy quality standards are among the highest in the world, helping to ensure the freshness and quality of all our dairy foods. To identify products made with milk from Canadian dairy producers, simply look for the little cow with the maple leaf on the packaging 🐄. This symbol means you are buying products made from one hundred percent Canadian milk; start with the best and experience the richness and flavour of Canadian dairy products in all our recipes.

⌣ Canadian Cheese

The use of cheese as a basic ingredient in cooking is a tradition that goes back some 300 years. Today, there are no fewer than 150 varieties of Canadian cheese. Whether you select cheese that's soft, ripened, fresh, sharp, hard or blue-veined, you can be sure it's big in the nutrition category. For example, protein contained in cheese helps build, maintain and repair body tissues. Throughout our carefully selected recipes, cheese, in all its endless variations, is showcased to bring out its wonderful taste and texture.

⌣ Milk: A Gourmet's Secret

The great chefs of the world use milk to make their soups creamier, their sauces smoother and their desserts more delicious. Kids love it in fruity milkshakes and frozen pops. Not only does it provide the necessary calcium for your body, but milk is also thirst-quenching, comforting and nutritious. Indulge in our creamy milk-based soups. On those cold winter nights, try serving a hot milk drink flavoured with chocolate or maple. From breakfast to dinner, milk is perfectly suited to a wide variety of dishes, from scrambled eggs and pancakes to pasta and fish.

⌣ The Crème de la Crème

Cream takes on different forms for a variety of flavours and culinary delights. It is just as suitable for salty meals as for sweets. A simple scoop of sour cream, for example, enhances the flavour of soup, potato salad or potatoes au gratin. There is nothing like the smoothness of coffee or table cream to make a quiche or pasta meal, or to make that cup of coffee complete. Last but not least, whipping cream adds a special touch to your favourite desserts. Discover all its richness in our savoury toppings and delicious sundae sauces.

⌣ Yogourt: A Healthy Pleasure

Yogourt is delicious however you choose to serve it. Well-suited to so many uses, it enables you to prepare dishes that are both lower in fat and higher in protein. Its various flavours add a nutritious and smooth touch to your meals. Yogourt blends in well with fresh fruit for the preparation of refreshing drinks. It can also be used to make amazing dips, to bring out the texture of your muffins and tarts, and let's not forget that a simple spoonful of yogourt, delicately placed on a hot steaming bowl of soup, adds a little touch of genius to your culinary creations.

⌣ A Touch of Butter for that Full Flavour

Nothing compares with butter when it comes to cooking and baking. Quite simply, it moisturizes, tenderizes, smooths, glazes and disperses the flavour of other foods. Butter is so flavourful that only a little makes all the difference. Whether on its own to grill fish or seafood, or blended with herbs to make a simple yet delicious accompaniment, there is no substitute for butter. When flavoured with honey, lime or coriander, butter will make you rediscover the taste of corn on the cob. And popcorn without butter just isn't popcorn.

⌣ Ice Cream in all its Richness

The rich, creamy texture and subtle flavour of ice cream make it one of the world's favourite treats. Offered in a wide variety of flavours and served in so many different ways, it is simply irresistible, especially to beat the heat of a hot summer day! Ice cream can be added to your milkshake recipes to prepare a refreshing drink, or simply serve it with fresh fruit to create a quick cool dessert.

SNACKS

Creamy Herb Dip

Creamy Herb Dip

1	pkg (125 g) Cream cheese, softened	1
¾ cup	yogourt *or* sour cream	175 mL
1 tbsp	*each* finely chopped green onion and parsley	15 mL
1 tsp	dried dill weed	5 mL
	seasoned salt	
	assorted crisp vegetables *or* crackers	

◄ In small mixer bowl, beat Cream cheese until smooth; gradually beat in yogourt or sour cream.

◄ Stir in onion, parsley and dill weed. Add salt to taste.

◄ Chill at least 1 hour to blend flavours. Serve with assorted vegetables or crackers for dipping.

Makes about 1²/3 cups (400 mL).
Preparation time: 10 minutes
Standing time: 1 hour

Creamy Seafood Dip: Omit parsley and dill weed. Add 1 tsp (5 mL) prepared horse-radish, ¾ tsp (3 mL) Worcestershire sauce and ¼ tsp (1 mL) hot pepper sauce. Stir in 1 cup (250 mL) drained, flaked crab meat *or* finely chopped cooked shrimp. *Makes about 2 cups (500 mL).*

Hot Cheddar Chili Bean Dip

2	cans (212 g *each*) chili con carne	2
1½ cups	shredded Canadian Cheddar cheese*	375 mL
	tortilla *or* corn chips	

* Or you can use shredded Canadian Jalapeño Havarti, Colby, Brick *or* Monterey Jack cheese.

◄ In medium saucepan, coarsely mash chili to break up beans; stir in Cheddar cheese.

◄ Cook and stir over medium-low heat until cheese is melted and mixture is heated through. Serve warm with tortilla chips for dipping.

Makes 2 cups (500 mL).
Preparation time: 5 minutes
Cooking time: 5 minutes

—**TIP**—
For a spicier dip add hot pepper sauce to taste.

Cheddar Potato Snacks

2	medium baking potatoes	2
	melted butter	
	salt and pepper	
1¼ cups	finely shredded Canadian Cheddar cheese	300 mL
6	slices side bacon, cooked, chopped	6
3 tbsp	finely chopped green onions	45 mL

◄ Preheat oven to 375°F (190°C).

◄ Cut thin slice from ends of each potato; discard. Cut potatoes into ¼-inch (5-mm) thick slices. Dry slices and place in single layer on lightly greased shallow baking sheet.

◄ Brush with melted butter; sprinkle with salt and pepper.

◄ Bake 10 minutes or until potatoes are tender. Combine Cheddar cheese, bacon and onions. Spoon onto potato slices. Bake 5 minutes longer or until cheese is melted.

Makes about 30 snacks.
Preparation time: 20 minutes
Baking time: 15 minutes

Swiss Cheese and Ham Potato Snacks:
Use finely shredded Canadian Swiss cheese instead of Cheddar cheese. Substitute ½ cup (125 mL) finely chopped cooked ham for bacon.

Oka and Mushroom Potato Snacks:
Use finely shredded Canadian Oka or Saint Paulin instead of Cheddar cheese. Instead of bacon add 1 cup (250 mL) finely chopped fresh mushrooms, sautéed in butter and seasoned to taste with salt and pepper.

Nacho Cheese Dip

2 tbsp	butter	30 mL
1	medium onion, chopped	1
1 cup	finely chopped tomatoes	250 mL
1 cup	milk	250 mL
1½ tbsp	flour	25 mL
1½ cups	shredded Canadian Cheddar cheese*	375 mL
2 tbsp	chopped jalapeño chilies or small hot peppers	30 mL
	hot pepper sauce or chili powder	
	tortilla chips	

* Or you can use shredded Canadian Brick, Farmers' or Monterey Jack cheese.

◄ In medium frypan, melt butter. Add onion and tomatoes; sauté over medium heat until onion is tender.

◄ In a small bowl, gradually stir milk into flour until smooth. Add to pan. Cook and stir over low heat until mixture boils and thickens. Remove from heat; add Cheddar cheese and stir until cheese is melted.

◄ Stir in chilies; add hot pepper sauce or chili powder to taste. Serve hot with tortilla chips for dipping.

Makes about 2½ cups (625 mL).
Preparation time: 15 minutes
Cooking time: 10 minutes

Pita Pizza Rounds

2	whole wheat pita bread rounds*	2
1	can (7½ oz/213 mL) pizza sauce	1
½ cup	chopped green pepper	125 mL
½ cup	thinly sliced pepperoni	125 mL
1	can (10 oz/284 mL) sliced mushrooms, drained	1
2 cups	shredded Canadian Mozzarella cheese**	500 mL
¼ cup	grated Canadian Parmesan cheese	50 mL

** Or you can use shredded Canadian Provolone *or* Fontina cheese.

◄ Preheat oven to 350°F (180°C).

◄ Separate each pita into two rounds. Place bread, hollow side up, on baking sheet.

◄ Spread equal amounts of pizza sauce over crusts. Distribute green pepper, pepperoni and mushrooms, or any of your favourite pizza ingredients, equally over the crusts. Top with Mozzarella cheese and sprinkle with Parmesan.

◄ Bake 20 minutes or until hot and bubbly.

* For thick crust pizzas, use 4 whole pita breads; do not separate them into halves.

Makes 4 servings.
Preparation time: 10 minutes
Baking time: 20 minutes

—TIP—

Use kitchen scissors to cut pizzas into bite-size wedges if desired. For extra zip, sprinkle each pizza with pickled jalapeño or hot banana pepper rings.

Spread equal amounts of pizza sauce over crusts.

Distribute green pepper, pepperoni and mushrooms equally over crusts.

Top with Mozzarella cheese and sprinkle with Parmesan.

Tex-Mex Popcorn

1/3 cup	butter, melted	75 mL
1 tsp	chili powder	5 mL
1/4 tsp	*each* hot pepper sauce and garlic powder	1 mL
10 cups	hot popped popcorn	2.5 L

◄ Combine butter, chili powder, pepper sauce and garlic powder. Drizzle over popcorn; toss to coat evenly. Serve immediately.

Makes about 10 cups (2.5 L).
Preparation time: 5 minutes

Parmesan Italian Popcorn

1/3 cup	butter, melted	75 mL
2 tbsp	grated Canadian Parmesan cheese	30 mL
1 tsp	dried basil	5 mL
1/2 tsp	dried oregano	2 mL
1/4 tsp	garlic powder	1 mL
10 cups	hot popped popcorn	2.5 L

◄ Combine butter, Parmesan cheese, basil, oregano and garlic powder. Drizzle over popcorn; toss to coat evenly. Serve immediately.

Makes about 10 cups (2.5 L).
Preparation time: 5 minutes

Taco Popcorn

1/3 cup	butter, melted	75 mL
2 tsp	taco seasoning mix	10 mL
10 cups	hot popped popcorn	2.5 L

◄ Combine butter and seasoning mix. Drizzle over popcorn; toss to coat evenly. Serve immediately.

Makes about 10 cups (2.5 L).
Preparation time: 5 minutes

Cheese 'n' Herb Spread

1	pkg (250 g) Cream cheese, softened	1
½ cup	butter, softened	125 mL
2 tbsp	fresh parsley	30 mL
1	garlic clove, chopped	1
¼ tsp	*each* salt and dried dill weed	1 mL
¼ tsp	*each* dried basil, thyme and marjoram leaves, crushed	1 mL
	Melba toast, crackers *or* French bread slices	

◄ In food processor fitted with metal blade, combine Cream cheese, butter, parsley, garlic, salt, dill weed, basil, thyme and marjoram. Cover and process until smooth.

◄ Pack into small crock or bowl. Let stand 1 hour to blend flavours. Serve with Melba toast, crackers or French bread.

Makes about 1¾ cups (425 mL).
Preparation time: 10 minutes
Standing time: 1 hour

Simple Cheesy Nachos

6 cups	tortilla chips	1.5 L
3 cups	shredded Canadian Cheddar cheese*	750 mL
	sliced pickled jalapeño pepper rings *or* salsa	
	sour cream	

* Or you can use shredded Canadian Brick, Farmers' *or* Monterey Jack cheese.

◄ Preheat oven to 400°F (200°C).

◄ Spread chips in foil-lined shallow baking pan. Top with Cheddar cheese.

◄ Bake 5 minutes or until cheese is melted. Garnish with jalapeño peppers and sour cream. Serve immediately.

Makes 6 to 8 servings.
Preparation time: 5 minutes
Baking time: 5 minutes

Cut each potato lengthwise into quarters.

Scoop out flesh, leaving 1/8-inch (3-mm) thick shell.

Brush skins, inside and out, with butter. Place cut-side-up in single layer on large baking sheet.

Cheesy Mexican Potato Skins

4	large baking potatoes	4
	melted butter	
	taco seasoning *or* chili powder	
2 cups	shredded Canadian Colby *or* Monterey Jack cheese	500 mL
1	can (7½ oz / 213 mL) taco sauce	1
1	small tomato, seeded and diced	1
2 tbsp	finely chopped parsley	30 mL

◄ Scrub potatoes and prick with fork. Bake at 400°F (200°C) 1 hour or until cooked; let cool.

◄ Cut each potato lengthwise into quarters. Scoop out flesh, leaving 1/8-inch (3-mm) thick shell; reserve scooped potato for other uses.

◄ Brush skins, inside and out, with butter. Place cut-side-up in single layer on large baking sheet. Increase oven to 500°F (260°C) and bake skins 12 minutes or until crisp.

◄ When done, sprinkle skins with taco seasoning and top with cheese. Return to oven until cheese is melted.

◄ In a small saucepan over medium heat, combine taco sauce, tomato and parsley. When hot, spoon over potato skins and serve.

Makes 16 snacks.
Preparation time: 20 minutes
Baking time: 1 hour and 15 minutes

Italian Baked Potato Skins: Prepare potato skins as above. Sprinkle lightly with dried oregano and top with a mixture of 1½ cups (375 mL) shredded Canadian Mozzarella *or* Provolone cheese and ¼ cup (50 mL) grated Canadian Parmesan cheese. Return to oven until cheeses are melted. Heat 1 can (7½ oz / 213 mL) pizza sauce. Spoon over potato skins and serve.

BEVERAGES

Very Berry Wake Up

Banana Breakfast Booster

2½ cups	cold milk	625 mL
2	eggs*	2
1	medium ripe banana, peeled, quartered	1
2 tbsp	liquid honey	30 mL
⅓ cup	frozen orange juice concentrate	75 mL

◄ Place milk, eggs, banana, honey and juice concentrate in blender container. Cover and blend at high speed until smooth.

Makes about 4 cups (1 L).
Preparation time: 5 minutes

Orange Pineapple Starter

1 cup	cold milk	250 mL
1	egg*	1
½ cup	crushed pineapple with juice	125 mL
¼ cup	frozen orange juice concentrate	50 mL
1 tbsp	sugar	15 mL

◄ Place milk, egg, pineapple, juice concentrate and sugar in blender container. Cover and blend at high speed until smooth.

Makes about 2 cups (500 mL).
Preparation time: 5 minutes

Very Berry Wake Up

2 cups	cold milk	500 mL
2	eggs*	2
1 cup	sliced strawberries	250 mL
¼ cup	sugar	50 mL

◄ Place milk, eggs, strawberries and sugar in blender container. Cover and blend at high speed until smooth.

Makes about 4 cups (1 L).
Preparation time: 5 minutes

* Be sure to use eggs with clean, uncracked shells.

Peanut Butter 'n' Honey Bee Shake

2	large scoops vanilla ice cream	2
1 cup	cold milk	250 mL
2 tbsp	liquid honey	30 mL
2 tbsp	peanut butter	30 mL

◄ Place ice cream, milk, honey and peanut butter in blender container. Cover and blend at high speed until smooth.

Makes about 2 1/4 cups (550 mL).
Preparation time: 5 minutes

Purple Dinosaur Shake

2	large scoops vanilla ice cream	2
1 cup	cold milk	250 mL
1/4 cup	frozen grape juice concentrate	50 mL

◄ Place ice cream, milk and juice concentrate in blender container. Cover and blend at high speed until smooth.

Makes about 2 1/4 cups (550 mL).
Preparation time: 5 minutes

Caramel Banana Shake-Up

1 cup	cold milk	250 mL
½	medium ripe banana, peeled, quartered	½
2	large scoops vanilla ice cream	2
2 tbsp	caramel *or* butterscotch sundae sauce	30 mL

◄ Place milk, banana, ice cream and sundae sauce in blender container. Cover and blend at high speed until smooth.

Makes about 3 cups (750 mL).
Preparation time: 5 minutes

Peachy Apricot Flip

1 cup	cold milk	250 mL
½ cup	canned sliced peaches, drained	125 mL
¼ cup	canned apricot halves, drained	50 mL
2	large scoops vanilla ice cream	2
	pinch ground nutmeg	

◄ Place milk, peaches, apricots, ice cream and nutmeg in blender container. Cover and blend at high speed until smooth.

Makes about 3 cups (750 mL).
Preparation time: 5 minutes

Frosty Apple

1 cup	cold milk	250 mL
1¼ cups	chilled sweetened apple sauce	300 mL
2	large scoops vanilla ice cream	2
¼ tsp	vanilla extract	1 mL
	pinch ground nutmeg	

◄ Place milk, apple sauce, ice cream, vanilla and nutmeg in blender container. Cover and blend at high speed until smooth.

Makes about 3 cups (750 mL).
Preparation time: 5 minutes

Watermelon Frappé

3 cups	seeded, cubed watermelon	750 mL
1½ cups	cold milk	375 mL
1	large scoop vanilla ice cream	1
1½ tsp	lemon juice	7 mL

◄ Place watermelon, milk, ice cream and lemon juice in blender container. Cover and blend at high speed until smooth.

Makes about 4 cups (1 L).
Preparation time: 5 minutes

Watermelon Frappé (left), Peachy Apricot Flip

Raspberry Smoothie

¾ cup	raspberry yogourt	175 mL
¾ cup	cold milk	175 mL
2 cups	raspberry sherbet	500 mL

◄ Place yogourt, milk and sherbet in blender container. Cover and blend at high speed until smooth.

Makes about 3 1/2 cups (875 mL).
Preparation time: 5 minutes

Honey Yogourt Sipper

1 cup	cold milk	250 mL
½ cup	vanilla *or* fruit-flavoured yogourt	125 mL
1	egg*	1
1 tbsp	liquid honey	15 mL

◄ Place milk, yogourt, egg and honey in blender container. Cover and blend at high speed until smooth.

* Be sure to use eggs with clean, uncracked shells.

Makes about 2 cups (500 mL).
Preparation time: 5 minutes

Apricot Fruit Flip

1 cup	cold milk	250 mL
½ cup	plain yogourt	125 mL
1	can (14 oz/398 mL) apricot halves*, drained	1
4	large ice cubes	4

◄ Place milk, yogourt, apricots and ice cubes in blender container. Cover and blend at high speed until smooth.

* Or you can use canned peaches, pineapple or mandarin oranges instead of apricots.

Makes about 3 cups (750 mL).
Preparation time: 5 minutes

Maple Hot Pot (left), P-Nutty Warm Up

Maple Hot Pot

4 cups	milk	1 L
½ cup	maple syrup	125 mL
2	cinnamon sticks	2
	ground cinnamon (optional)	

◄ In large saucepan, combine milk, maple syrup and cinnamon sticks. Cook and stir over medium heat until heated through. Pour into mugs and sprinkle with cinnamon, if desired.

Makes about 4 cups (1 L).
Preparation time: 10 minutes

Spiced Hot Chocolate

2 tbsp	unsweetened cocoa powder	30 mL
4 tsp	sugar	20 mL
½ tsp	ground cinnamon	2 mL
3 cups	milk	750 mL
	whipped cream (optional)	

◄ In large saucepan, combine cocoa, sugar and cinnamon. Add just enough milk to make a smooth paste then stir in remaining milk. Cook and stir over medium heat until heated through. Pour into mugs and top with whipped cream, if desired.

Makes about 3 cups (750 mL).
Preparation time: 10 minutes

P-Nutty Warm Up

½ cup	liquid honey	125 mL
⅓ cup	smooth peanut butter	75 mL
4 cups	milk	1 L
	ground nutmeg (optional)	

◄ In large saucepan, combine honey and peanut butter until smooth. Gradually stir in milk. Cook and stir over medium heat until heated through. Pour into mugs and sprinkle with nutmeg, if desired.

Makes about 5 cups (1.25 L).
Preparation time: 10 minutes

Choco-Minty Milk

4 cups	cold milk	1 L
¾ cup	chocolate sundae sauce	175 mL
½ tsp	peppermint extract	2 mL

◄ Place milk, sundae sauce and peppermint extract in blender container. Cover and blend at high speed until smooth.

Makes about 5 cups (1.25 L).
Preparation time: 5 minutes

Chocolate Orange Blossom

2 cups	cold chocolate milk	500 mL
2 tbsp	frozen orange juice concentrate	30 mL

◄ Place milk and juice concentrate in blender container. Cover and blend at high speed until smooth.

Makes about 2 cups (500 mL).
Preparation time: 5 minutes

Caribbean Cooler

1 cup	cold milk	250 mL
½	medium ripe banana, peeled, quartered	½
¼ cup	frozen orange, banana and pineapple juice concentrate	50 mL

◄ Place milk, banana and juice concentrate in blender container. Cover and blend at high speed until smooth.

Makes about 2 cups (500 mL).
Preparation time: 5 minutes

Rio Shake

2 cups	cold milk	500 mL
1	medium ripe banana, peeled, quartered	1
4	scoops coffee ice cream	4

◄ Place milk, banana and ice cream in blender container. Cover and blend at high speed until smooth.

Makes about 4 cups (1 L).
Preparation time: 5 minutes

Creamy Frosted Coffee

1 cup	cold whipping cream	250 mL
¼ cup	icing sugar	50 mL
1 cup	cold coffee	250 mL
4	scoops coffee ice cream	4
	toasted slivered almonds	

◄ Beat whipping cream until soft peaks form. Add icing sugar and beat until stiff. Divide coffee evenly among four tall glasses. Divide whipped cream among the glasses, making sure it touches glass all around. Top with ice cream; sprinkle with almonds.

Makes about 5 cups (1.25 L).
Preparation time: 10 minutes

Chilly Café au Lait

2 tsp	instant coffee	10 mL
¼ cup	boiling water	50 mL
2 tbsp	sugar	30 mL
2 cups	cold milk	500 mL

◄ Combine coffee, boiling water and sugar until dissolved; cool completely. Stir in milk.

Makes about 2 cups (500 mL).
Preparation time: 15 minutes

Creamy Frosted Coffee (left), Chilly Café au Lait

SOUPS
AND SAUCES

Hearty Split Pea Soup

2 cups	dried yellow split peas	500 mL
6 cups	water	1.5 L
2 cups	chopped cooked ham	500 mL
1 cup	shredded carrot	250 mL
¾ cup	chopped onion	175 mL
¼ cup	butter	50 mL
2 cups	milk	500 mL
¼ tsp	cayenne pepper	1 mL
	salt and pepper	

◄ In large saucepan, combine peas and water. Bring to a boil over medium-high heat; boil 2 minutes. Remove from heat, cover and let stand 1 hour. (Do not change water.)

◄ Add ham, carrot, onion and butter to peas. Bring to a boil. Reduce heat, cover and simmer 35 minutes or until peas are tender. Stir in milk and cayenne pepper. Add salt and pepper to taste. Reheat and serve.

Makes 8 servings.
Preparation time: 10 minutes
Standing time: 1 hour
Cooking time: 35 minutes

— TIP —

Dried green split peas or lentils also work well in this recipe. You can freeze any leftover soup for up to two months.

Cheddar Fish Chowder

6	slices bacon, chopped	6
1/2 cup	*each* thinly sliced celery and chopped onion	125 mL
1	pkg (400 g) frozen fish fillets, partially thawed	1
2 cups	diced, peeled potatoes, uncooked	500 mL
2	cans (10 oz/284 mL *each*) chicken broth	2
1/4 tsp	ground thyme	1 mL
1	bay leaf	1
1/2 cup	butter	125 mL
1/3 cup	all-purpose flour	75 mL
4 cups	milk	1 L
2 cups	shredded Canadian Cheddar cheese*	500 mL

◄ In large saucepan, cook bacon until crisp. Remove bacon with slotted spoon and set aside. Over medium heat sauté celery and onion in bacon drippings until tender.

◄ Cut fish into 1/2-inch (1-cm) pieces. Add to saucepan along with potatoes, chicken broth, thyme and bay leaf. Bring to a boil. Reduce heat, cover and simmer 10 minutes or until potatoes are tender.

◄ Meanwhile, melt butter in medium saucepan. Blend in flour and gradually stir in milk. Cook and stir over medium heat until mixture boils and thickens. Remove from heat, add Cheddar cheese and stir until cheese is melted.

◄ Stir into fish mixture. Discard bay leaf and season to taste with salt and pepper. Top with reserved bacon and serve.

Makes 8 to 10 servings.
Preparation time: 10 minutes
Cooking time: 25 minutes

* Or you can use shredded Canadian Gouda, Fontina, Brick *or* Colby cheese.

Cauliflower 'n' Cheddar Soup

3 tbsp	butter	45 mL
2/3 cup	chopped onion	150 mL
5 cups	coarsely chopped cauliflower	1.25 L
2	cans (10 oz/284 mL each) chicken broth	2
3 cups	milk	750 mL
1/3 cup	all-purpose flour	75 mL
2 1/2 cups	shredded Canadian Cheddar cheese*	625 mL
1/4 cup	chopped parsley	50 mL
	salt and pepper	

◄ In large saucepan, melt butter. Sauté onion until tender. Stir in cauliflower and chicken broth. Bring to a boil over medium-high heat. Reduce heat, cover and simmer 12 minutes or until cauliflower is tender.

◄ In a bowl, gradually stir milk into flour until smooth. Add to saucepan. Cook and stir over medium heat until mixture boils and thickens. Remove from heat, add cheese and parsley and stir until cheese is melted. Add salt and pepper to taste.

Makes 8 servings.
Preparation time: 10 minutes
Cooking time: 25 minutes

* Or you can use shredded Canadian Swiss, Gouda, Mozzarella *or* Colby cheese.

Canadiana Cheddar Cheese Soup

3 tbsp	butter	45 mL
¼ cup	finely chopped onion	50 mL
¼ cup	finely grated carrot	50 mL
¼ cup	all-purpose flour	50 mL
1 tbsp	chicken bouillon mix	15 mL
½ tsp	*each* paprika and dry mustard	2 mL
4 cups	milk	1 L
2 cups	shredded Canadian Cheddar cheese	500 mL
	paprika to taste	

◄ In medium saucepan, melt butter. Sauté onion and carrot until tender.

◄ Blend in flour, bouillon mix, paprika and mustard. Gradually stir in milk. Cook and stir over medium heat until mixture boils and thickens.

◄ Remove from heat, add Cheddar cheese and stir until cheese is melted. Sprinkle each portion with more paprika and serve.

Makes 4 servings.
Preparation time: 10 minutes
Cooking time: 10 minutes

Double Cheese Soup: Use 1½ cups (375 mL) shredded Canadian Mozzarella and ½ cup (125 mL) grated Canadian Parmesan instead of Cheddar cheese.

Great Gouda Soup: Use shredded Canadian Gouda instead of Cheddar cheese.

Blend flour, bouillon mix,
paprika and mustard into
sautéed onion and carrot.

Gradually stir in milk.

Remove from heat, add
Cheddar cheese and stir
until cheese is melted.

Havarti-Topped Golden Carrot Soup

¼ cup	butter	50 mL
½ cup	chopped onion	125 mL
3 cups	thinly sliced carrots	750 mL
3 cups	water	750 mL
¼ cup	uncooked long grain rice	50 mL
1 tbsp	chicken bouillon mix	15 mL
2 cups	milk	500 mL
	salt and pepper	
	buttered croutons	
1 cup	shredded Canadian Havarti cheese*	250 mL
	chopped parsley	

* Or you can use shredded Canadian Cheddar, Colby, Brick *or* Gouda cheese.

◄ In large saucepan, melt butter. Sauté onion until tender. Add carrots, water, rice and bouillon mix. Bring to a boil over medium-high heat. Reduce heat, cover and simmer 20 minutes or until carrots are tender and rice is cooked.

◄ Pour mixture in batches into blender container. Cover and blend until smooth. Return mixture to saucepan. Stir in milk; season with salt and pepper to taste. Reheat to serving temperature.

◄ Ladle into bowls and top with buttered croutons, Havarti cheese and parsley.

Makes 6 servings.
Preparation time: 10 minutes
Cooking time: 20 minutes

Buttered Croutons: Toss 1½ cups (375 mL) bread cubes in 3 tbsp (45 mL) melted butter. Bake at 350°F (180°C) 7 minutes. Turn cubes over; bake 7 minutes longer. *Makes about 1½ cups (375 mL).*

Cheddar Sauce Suprême

2 tbsp	butter	30 mL
2 tbsp	flour	30 mL
1 tsp	chicken bouillon mix	5 mL
	pinch dry mustard	
1½ cups	milk	375 mL
1½ cups	shredded Canadian Cheddar cheese	375 mL
	salt and pepper	

◄ In medium saucepan, melt butter. Blend in flour, bouillon mix and mustard. Gradually stir in milk. Cook and stir over medium heat until mixture boils and thickens. Remove from heat.

◄ Add Cheddar cheese and stir until cheese is melted. Season with salt and pepper to taste. Serve over your favourite vegetables or meat.

Makes about 2 cups (500 mL).
Preparation time: 5 minutes
Cooking time: 7 minutes

Swiss Mornay Sauce: Increase butter and flour to 3 tbsp (45 mL) *each*, increase milk to 2 cups (500 mL). Use ½ cup (125 mL) shredded Canadian Swiss instead of Cheddar cheese. Serve over chicken breasts, poached eggs, or any kind of vegetable.

Creamy Mushroom Sauce

2 tbsp	butter	30 mL
2 cups	sliced fresh mushrooms	500 mL
2 tbsp	finely chopped onion	30 mL
2 tbsp	flour	30 mL
1 tsp	chicken bouillon mix	5 mL
1½ cups	milk	375 mL
	salt and pepper	

◄ In medium saucepan, melt butter. Sauté mushrooms and onion until tender and liquid has evaporated. Blend in flour and bouillon mix. Gradually stir in milk. Cook and stir over medium heat until mixture boils and thickens. Add salt and pepper to taste. Serve over meatloaf, meatballs, or any kind of vegetable.

Makes about 2¼ cups (300 mL).
Preparation time: 10 minutes
Cooking time: 10 minutes

Easy Tzatziki

1 cup	plain yogourt	250 mL
1 cup	shredded seedless cucumber, squeezed dry	250 mL
1	garlic clove, minced	1
¼ tsp	sugar	1 mL
	salt and pepper	

◄ In small bowl, combine yogourt, cucumber, garlic and sugar. Add salt and pepper to taste.

◄ Let stand 1 hour to blend flavours. Serve with souvlaki or grilled chicken sandwiches.

Makes about 1 1/3 cups (325 mL).
Preparation time: 10 minutes
Standing time: 1 hour

Variation: For a thicker sauce, start with yogourt cheese: line a 6-inch (15-cm) strainer with a double layer of cheesecloth; place over bowl. Add 2 cups (500 mL) plain yogourt (with no gelatin or starch added) to strainer. Cover and refrigerate 24 hours to drain. Discard whey liquid. *Makes about 1 cup (250 mL).*

Sauté onions over medium heat until tender. Stir in water and bouillon mix.

Gradually stir milk into flour until smooth. Add to saucepan.

Remove from heat, add 3/4 cup (175 mL) of the Swiss cheese and stir until cheese is melted.

Creamy Swiss Onion Soup

¼ cup	butter	50 mL
3 cups	quartered, thinly sliced onions	750 mL
1½ cups	water	375 mL
1½ tbsp	chicken bouillon mix	25 mL
1¾ cups	milk	425 mL
¼ cup	all-purpose flour	50 mL
1½ cups	shredded Canadian Swiss cheese*, divided	375 mL
	salt and pepper	
	buttered croutons	

* Or you can use shredded Canadian Cheddar, Mozzarella *or* Provolone cheese.

◄ In large saucepan, melt butter. Sauté onions over medium heat until tender. Stir in water and bouillon mix. Bring to a boil over medium-high heat. Reduce heat, cover and simmer 15 minutes.

◄ In a bowl, gradually stir milk into flour until smooth. Add to saucepan. Cook and stir over medium heat until mixture boils and thickens. Remove from heat, add ¾ cup (175 mL) of the Swiss cheese and stir until cheese is melted. Season with salt and pepper to taste.

◄ Ladle into ovenproof soup bowls and sprinkle with buttered croutons. Top with remaining Swiss cheese. Broil until cheese is melted and serve.

Makes 4 servings.
Preparation time: 10 minutes
Cooking time: 10 minutes

Buttered Croutons: Toss 1½ cups (375 mL) bread cubes in 3 tbsp (45 mL) melted butter. Bake in 350°F (180°C) oven 7 minutes. Turn cubes over and bake 7 minutes longer. *Makes about 1½ cups (375 mL).*

Swiss Potato Soup

2 tbsp	butter	30 mL
¼ cup	chopped onion	50 mL
2 cups	diced, peeled potatoes, uncooked	500 mL
1	can (10 oz/284 mL) chicken broth	1
	pinch ground marjoram	
3 cups	milk	750 mL
2 tbsp	flour	30 mL
1 tbsp	chopped parsley	15 mL
	salt and pepper	
1 cup	shredded Canadian Swiss cheese*	250 mL

◄ In large saucepan, melt butter. Sauté onion until tender. Add potatoes, chicken broth, and marjoram. Bring to a boil over medium-high heat. Reduce heat, cover and simmer 10 minutes or until potatoes are tender.

◄ In a bowl, gradually stir milk into flour until smooth. Add to saucepan. Cook and stir over medium heat until mixture boils and thickens. Stir in parsley. Season with salt and pepper to taste.

◄ Ladle into bowls and top with Swiss cheese. Swirl cheese through soup and serve.

Makes 4 servings.
Preparation time: 10 minutes
Cooking time: 20 minutes

* Or you can use shredded Canadian Cheddar, Gouda, Colby, Brick *or* Havarti cheese.

Creamy Brie and Fresh Mushroom Soup

3 cups	thinly sliced fresh mushrooms	750 mL
½ cup	chopped onion	125 mL
1 tbsp	chicken bouillon mix	15 mL
1 cup	water	250 mL
¼ cup	butter	50 mL
¼ cup	all-purpose flour	50 mL
	pinch poultry seasoning	
3 cups	milk	750 mL
	salt and pepper	
4 oz	Canadian Brie cheese*, thinly sliced	125 g

* Or you can use shredded Canadian Swiss, Mozzarella *or* Provolone cheese.

◄ In medium saucepan, combine mushrooms, onion, bouillon mix and water. Bring to a boil over medium-high heat. Reduce heat, cover and simmer 15 minutes.

◄ In large saucepan, melt butter. Blend in flour and poultry seasoning. Gradually stir in milk. Cook and stir over medium heat until mixture boils and thickens. Stir in undrained mushroom mixture. Add salt and pepper to taste.

◄ To serve, divide Brie cheese among four soup bowls; top with hot soup. Stir melted cheese through soup.

Makes 4 servings.
Preparation time: 15 minutes
Cooking time: 25 minutes

─TIP─

Look for firm, fleshy mushrooms with no discolouration or bruises. Store, unwashed, in a paper bag in the refrigerator for up to five days.

SANDWICHES AND SALADS

Pinwheel Salad

8 cups	crisp torn salad greens	2 L
1½ cups	diced Canadian Havarti cheese*	375 mL
1½ cups	diced cooked chicken	375 mL
1 cup	*each* diced seeded tomato and green pepper	250 mL
10	slices side bacon, crisp-cooked, crumbled	10
3	hard-cooked eggs, peeled, diced	3
⅓ cup	sliced green onions	75 mL

Tangy Dressing:

6 tbsp	white wine vinegar	90 mL
½ cup	vegetable oil	125 mL
	pinch garlic powder	
	salt and pepper to taste	

* Or you can use diced Canadian Farmers', Brick *or* Colby cheese.

◄ Place greens in large salad bowl. Arrange Havarti cheese, chicken, tomato, green pepper, bacon and eggs in separate wedge-shaped sections on top of greens.

◄ Sprinkle green onions over centre of bowl. Cover and refrigerate until ready to serve.

◄ Meanwhile, combine Tangy Dressing ingredients in small jar. Cover and shake well.

◄ Pour over salad, toss and serve.

Makes 4 to 5 servings.
Preparation time: 15 minutes

Colby Bean Buns

½ lb	lean ground beef	250 g
1	can (14 oz/398 mL) beans with pork	1
¼ cup	bottled barbecue sauce	50 mL
4	hamburger buns	4
3 cups	shredded Canadian Colby cheese*, divided	750 mL

* Or you can use shredded Canadian Cheddar, Brick, Farmers' or Monterey Jack cheese.

◄ In large frypan, cook meat over medium heat and drain. Add beans and barbecue sauce; bring to a boil over medium-high heat. Reduce heat and simmer, uncovered, 5 minutes or until heated through.

◄ Split buns and toast under broiler. Sprinkle ¼ cup (50 mL) of the Colby cheese on each half bun and broil until cheese is melted. Spoon equal amounts of hot bean mixture onto each half bun. Top with remaining 1 cup (250 mL) Colby cheese. Broil until cheese is melted and serve.

Makes 8 servings.
Preparation time: 20 minutes
Cooking time: 3 to 4 minutes

Variation: Lean ground pork, chicken or turkey may be substituted for beef. Hot dog buns work as well as hamburger buns.

Swiss Cabbage Slaw

3 cups	coarsely shredded green cabbage	750 mL
1 cup	coarsely shredded red cabbage	250 mL
1 cup	sliced celery	250 mL
½	pkg (200 g) sliced Canadian Swiss cheese*	½
¼ cup	*each* chopped green onions and parsley	50 mL
½ cup	mayonnaise *or* salad dressing	125 mL
½ cup	sour cream	125 mL
	salt and pepper	

* Or you can use sliced Canadian Mozzarella *or* Havarti cheese.

◄ In large salad bowl, combine green and red cabbage, celery, Swiss cheese, onions and parsley.

◄ In small bowl, stir together mayonnaise and sour cream. Pour dressing over cabbage mixture and toss well to coat. Season with salt and pepper to taste. Chill 1 hour to blend flavours.

Makes 6 servings.
Preparation time: 15 minutes
Chilling time: 1 hour

—TIP—

To "shred" cabbage, quarter and core one head and cut crosswise with sharp knife into thin strips.

Greek Pasta Salad

¼ cup	vegetable oil	50 mL
1½ tbsp	lemon juice	25 mL
2 tsp	fresh oregano leaves	10 mL
1	garlic clove, chopped	1
1½ cups	penne pasta, cooked, drained	375 mL
1 cup	crumbled Canadian Feta cheese*	250 mL
1 cup	*each* diced tomato and seedless cucumber	250 mL
½ cup	*each* sliced pitted black olives and green pepper	125 mL
2 tbsp	*each* chopped parsley and green onions	30 mL
	salt and pepper	

* Or you can use diced Canadian Brick *or* Havarti cheese.

◄ In blender container, place oil, lemon juice, oregano and garlic. Cover and blend at high speed until mixture is creamy.

◄ In large salad bowl, combine pasta, Feta cheese, tomato, cucumber, olives, green pepper, parsley and onions. Pour in creamy dressing and toss well. Add salt and pepper to taste. Chill at least 1 hour to blend flavours.

Makes 4 main dish or 8 side dish servings.
Preparation time: 15 minutes
Chilling time: 1 hour

—TIP—

Add variety to this salad by using different shapes of pasta, such as rotini, bowties or elbow macaroni. You can use 1 tsp (5 mL) dried oregano instead of fresh oregano.

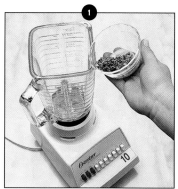

1

In blender container, place oil, lemon juice, oregano and garlic. Cover and blend until mixture is creamy.

2

In large salad bowl, combine pasta, Feta cheese, tomato, cucumber, olives, green pepper, parsley and onions.

3

Pour in creamy dressing and toss well. Add salt and pepper to taste.

Garden Patch Pitas

1½ cups	Cottage cheese*	375 mL
½ cup	diced seedless cucumber	125 mL
½ cup	diced *or* shredded carrot	125 mL
¼ cup	mayonnaise *or* salad dressing	50 mL
2 tbsp	finely chopped green onion	30 mL
1 tbsp	vinegar	15 mL
½ tsp	dried dill weed	2 mL
	salt and pepper	
2	pita bread rounds, halved	2
	leaf lettuce	

◄ In medium bowl, combine Cottage cheese, cucumber, carrot, mayonnaise, onion, vinegar and dill weed; toss lightly to combine. Season with salt and pepper to taste.

◄ Partially open each pita pocket, line with lettuce and fill with Cottage cheese-vegetable mixture.

Makes 2 servings.
Preparation time: 15 minutes

* Or you can use Canadian Ricotta cheese.

Egg Salad Pitas

6	hard-boiled eggs, peeled, chopped	6
½ cup	mayonnaise *or* salad dressing	125 mL
⅓ cup	finely chopped celery	75 mL
2 tbsp	finely chopped green onion	30 mL
1½ cups	shredded Canadian Cheddar cheese*	375 mL
	salt and pepper	
4	pita bread rounds, halved	4
	alfalfa sprouts	

◄ In medium bowl, combine eggs, mayonnaise, celery and onions. Stir in Cheddar cheese. Add salt and pepper to taste.

◄ Partially open each pita bread half and line with sprouts. Divide egg mixture evenly among pita pockets.

Makes 4 servings.
Preparation time: 15 minutes

* Or you can use shredded Canadian Colby *or* Gouda cheese.

Taco Salad Bowls

1 lb	lean ground beef	500 g
1	pkg (35 g) taco seasoning mix	1
6 cups	shredded iceberg lettuce	1.5 L
1	small green pepper, diced	1
¼ cup	sliced green onions	50 mL
2 cups	diced Canadian Colby cheese*	500 mL
2	medium tomatoes, seeded, diced	2
½	medium seedless cucumber, diced	½
	bottled Ranch-style salad dressing	

* Or you can use diced Canadian Farmers', Brick, Havarti *or* Gouda cheese.

◄ In large frypan, cook beef over medium heat and drain. Sprinkle seasoning mix over beef. Add ¾ cup (175 mL) water to pan and mix until well-combined. Cook and stir over medium heat until mixture comes to a boil. Remove from heat and let cool.

◄ Just before serving, toss together lettuce, green pepper and green onions. Divide equally among individual salad bowls. Top with rows of cooked meat mixture, Colby cheese, tomatoes and cucumber. Serve with Ranch-style dressing.

Makes 4 to 6 servings.
Preparation time: 15 minutes
Cooking time: 10 minutes

Variation: Serve in edible taco salad bowls. For each bowl, lightly brush one side of a flour tortilla with melted butter. Ease tortilla, buttered side down, into an ovenproof mixing bowl, gently pleating edges. Bake at 350°F (180°C) 15 minutes. Remove shell from bowl; cool completely.

Open-Faced BLT Sandwiches

1 tbsp	butter	15 mL
1 tbsp	flour	15 mL
¼ tsp	Worcestershire sauce	1 mL
¾ cup	milk	175 mL
1 cup	shredded Canadian Cheddar cheese*	250 mL
	salt and pepper	
	leaf lettuce	
12	tomato slices	12
12	slices side bacon, cooked	12
6	slices French bread, toasted if desired, buttered	6

◄ In small saucepan, melt butter. Blend in flour and Worcestershire sauce. Gradually stir in milk. Cook and stir over medium heat until mixture boils and thickens; remove from heat.

◄ Add Cheddar cheese and stir until cheese is melted. Season with salt and pepper to taste.

◄ For each serving, place lettuce, two slices of tomato and two slices of bacon on each piece of bread; top with cheese sauce.

Makes 6 servings.
Preparation time: 10 minutes
Cooking time: 10 minutes

—TIP—

You can use split, toasted and buttered English muffins instead of French bread.

* Or you can use shredded Canadian Colby *or* Gouda cheese.

1

Spread butter on one side of each tortilla.

2

Arrange sliced Brick and Colby cheeses over tortillas.

3

Spoon Fresh Tomato Salsa over hot quesadillas.

Mexican Quesadillas

8	flour tortillas	8
	butter	
8 oz	Canadian Brick cheese*, thinly sliced	250 g
8 oz	Canadian Colby cheese*, thinly sliced	250 g

Fresh Tomato Salsa:

1	large fresh tomato, diced	1
1	small white *or* red onion, diced	1
1	jalapeño pepper, seeded and diced	1
2-3 tbsp	chopped fresh coriander	30-45 mL
1 tbsp	fresh lime juice	15 mL
	salt and pepper to taste	

◄ Preheat oven to 400°F (200°C).

◄ Spread butter on one side of each tortilla. Place tortillas, buttered side up, on ungreased baking sheets. Bake 5 minutes; remove from oven.

◄ Arrange sliced Brick and Colby cheeses over tortillas. Bake 5 minutes longer or until cheeses are melted. Remove from oven.

◄ Meanwhile, combine all salsa ingredients in a medium bowl and stir well. Spoon over hot quesadillas and serve.

Makes 8 servings.
Preparation time: 10 minutes
Baking time: 10 minutes

— **TIP** —

If time is short, you can use prepared mild, medium or hot salsa instead of Fresh Tomato Salsa.

* Or you can use thinly sliced Jalapeño Havarti, Monterey Jack *and/or* Mozzarella cheese.

Cheese Steak Sandwiches

3 tbsp	butter	45 mL
2 tbsp	flour	30 mL
¾ cup	milk	175 mL
1 cup	shredded Canadian Cheddar cheese*	250 mL
1	large onion, thinly sliced	1
1	large green pepper, thinly sliced	1
1 lb	minute steaks, cut in thin strips	500 g
	salt and pepper	
4	large crusty rolls, split in half	4

* Or you can use shredded Canadian Colby, Brick, Farmers' or Gouda cheese.

◄ In medium saucepan, melt 2 tbsp (30 mL) butter. Blend in flour. Gradually stir in milk. Cook and stir over medium heat until mixture boils and thickens. Remove from heat, add Cheddar cheese and stir until cheese is melted. Cover and keep warm.

◄ In large frypan, heat remaining butter. Sauté onion and green pepper until tender; remove from pan with slotted spoon and keep warm. Add more butter to pan, if necessary, and sauté meat until cooked as desired. Return vegetables to pan and heat through. Add salt and pepper to taste.

◄ Distribute meat and vegetable mixture over bottom half of each roll. Spoon about ¼ cup (50 mL) cheese sauce over each serving. Replace top of roll.

Makes 4 servings.
Preparation time: 10 minutes
Cooking time: 20 minutes

Apple Cheese Toss

1 cup	sour cream	250 mL
¼ cup	liquid honey	50 mL
2 tsp	lemon juice	10 mL
4 cups	diced, cored red apples	1 L
1¼ cups	diced Canadian Colby cheese*	300 mL
1 cup	sliced celery	250 mL
½ cup	walnut pieces	125 mL
	leaf lettuce	

* Or you can use diced Canadian Cheddar, Havarti, Brick *or* Farmers' cheese.

◄ In small bowl, combine sour cream, honey and lemon juice. Chill dressing at least 1 hour to blend flavours.

◄ Just before serving, combine apples, Colby cheese, celery and nuts in large bowl. Pour in dressing and toss lightly to combine. Spoon into lettuce-lined bowl and serve.

Makes 6 servings.
Preparation time: 10 minutes
Chilling time: 1 hour

— TIP —

Sprinkle diced apples with lemon juice to prevent discolouring.

EGGS

Italian Spinach Ricotta Pie

8	slices side bacon, chopped	8
2 cups	chopped fresh mushrooms	500 mL
1/3 cup	finely chopped onion	75 mL
1	pkg (300 g) frozen chopped spinach, thawed, well drained	1
1	container (475 g) Canadian Ricotta cheese	1
1 cup	shredded Canadian Swiss cheese*	250 mL
1/2 cup	grated Canadian Parmesan cheese	125 mL
1 tsp	dried oregano	5 mL
1/4 tsp	salt	1 mL
1	egg	1
	pastry for a double crust pie	
1	can (7 1/2 oz/213 mL) pizza sauce, heated	1

* Or you can use shredded Canadian Mozzarella, Provolone *or* Fontina cheese.

◄ Preheat oven to 425°F (220°C).

◄ In large frypan, cook bacon until crisp and set aside. Drain all but 1 tbsp (15 mL) of drippings. Sauté mushrooms and onions in drippings until tender and liquid has evaporated.

◄ In large bowl, combine spinach, Ricotta, Swiss and Parmesan cheeses with bacon, mushroom mixture, oregano, salt and egg; mix well.

◄ On lightly floured board roll out two-thirds of the pastry and line a 9-inch (23-cm) pie plate, leaving 1/2-inch (1-cm) over-lapping the edge. Spoon filling evenly over pastry. Roll out remaining pastry and cover pie. Seal and flute edges; cut several steam vents.

◄ Bake 25 minutes or until cooked and browned. Let stand 10 minutes. Cut pie into wedges and serve with hot pizza sauce.

Makes 6 servings.
Preparation time: 15 minutes
Baking time: 25 minutes

Baked Cheddar Strata

8	slices day-old bread	8
	soft butter	
2 cups	shredded Canadian Cheddar cheese*	500 mL
5	eggs	5
3 cups	milk	750 mL
½ tsp	salt	2 mL
¼ tsp	ground black pepper	1 mL

* Or you can use shredded Canadian Colby, Oka *or* Swiss cheese.

◄ Preheat oven to 350°F (180°C).

◄ Trim crusts from bread and butter lightly. Arrange 4 slices in bottom of greased 9-inch (23-cm) square baking dish. Sprinkle half of Cheddar cheese over bread. Repeat with remaining bread and cheese to form a second layer.

◄ In medium bowl, beat eggs well. Stir in milk, salt and pepper. Pour over bread and cheese. Bake 35 minutes or until knife inserted in centre comes out clean.

Makes 6 servings.
Preparation time: 10 minutes
Baking time: 35 minutes

— TIP —

This recipe makes great use of leftover bread. Whole wheat, egg or rye bread works equally well. For a complete meal, spoon diced sautéed vegetables over each serving.

Cheese Omelet

2	eggs	2
2 tbsp	water	30 mL
	pinch *each* dried basil and chives	
1 tsp	butter	5 mL
½ cup	shredded Canadian Cheddar cheese	125 mL

◄ In small bowl, lightly beat eggs. Beat in water, basil and chives.

◄ Melt butter in 8-inch (20-cm) non-stick frypan until sizzling hot. Pour in egg mixture and swirl gently. Cook over low heat, using a spatula to move the cooked portion to the centre of the pan, tilting and rotating the pan to allow uncooked portion to flow into empty spaces.

◄ Fill one side of the omelet with Cheddar cheese. Slip spatula under unfilled side, fold over and serve.

Makes 1 serving.
Preparation time: 5 minutes
Cooking time: about 8 minutes

Swiss Ham Omelet: Substitute shredded Canadian Swiss for Cheddar cheese and sprinkle cheese with ¼ cup (50 mL) chopped cooked ham before folding omelet.

Mushroom Brie Omelet: Substitute thinly sliced Canadian Brie *or* Camembert for Cheddar cheese and sprinkle cheese with sautéed mushrooms before folding omelet.

Versatile Quiche

1	frozen (9-inch/23-cm) deep dish pie shell	1
1½ cups	shredded Canadian Swiss cheese*	375 mL
1	can (7½ oz/213 g) salmon**, drained, flaked	1
1 tbsp	*each* finely chopped onion, celery and parsley	15 mL
1 tbsp	flour	15 mL
½ tsp	salt	2 mL
3	eggs, beaten	3
1 cup	light *or* table cream	250 mL
1 tbsp	grated Canadian Parmesan cheese	15 mL

* Or you can use shredded Canadian Cheddar, Colby, Farmers', Brick *or* Gouda cheese.

◄ Preheat oven to 375°F (190°C).

◄ Place pie shell on baking sheet and let thaw 10 minutes.

◄ In medium bowl, toss together Swiss cheese, salmon, onion, celery, parsley, flour and salt. Spoon into unbaked pie shell.

◄ Combine eggs and cream; pour over Swiss cheese mixture. Sprinkle with Parmesan cheese.

◄ Bake 35 minutes or until knife inserted into centre comes out clean.

** Or substitute 1 can (6½ oz/184 g) tuna, flaked ham *or* flaked chicken for salmon.

Makes 6 servings.
Preparation time: 15 minutes
Baking time: 35 minutes

Swiss Bacon 'n' Mushroom Frittata

8	slices side bacon, chopped	8
3 cups	sliced fresh mushrooms	750 mL
1/3 cup	sliced green onions	75 mL
1 tbsp	flour	15 mL
1/2 tsp	salt	2 mL
6	eggs	6
3/4 cup	milk	175 mL
2 cups	shredded Canadian Swiss cheese*, divided	500 mL
1 tbsp	grated Canadian Parmesan cheese	15 mL

* Or you can use shredded Canadian Havarti, Colby *or* Cheddar cheese.

◄ In large non-stick frypan, cook bacon until crisp. Drain, reserving 1 tbsp (15 mL) drippings; set bacon aside. Sauté mushrooms and onions in reserved drippings until tender and liquid has evaporated. Add flour and salt to pan; toss to coat.

◄ In large bowl, lightly beat eggs. Stir in milk. Add sautéed vegetables and 1 1/2 cups (375 mL) of the Swiss cheese. Pour into frypan and cover.

◄ Cook over low heat 20 minutes or until set. Remove cover. Sprinkle with remaining 1/2 cup (125 mL) Swiss cheese, Parmesan cheese and reserved bacon. Broil until cheese is melted.

Makes 4 servings.
Preparation time: 15 minutes
Cooking time: 20 minutes

—TIP—

If frypan handle is not ovenproof, wrap it completely with aluminum foil to protect it from the heat of the broiler.

Cook bacon until crisp.

Sauté mushrooms and onions in reserved drippings until tender.

Add flour and salt to pan; toss to coat.

Lightly beat eggs and stir in milk.

Add sautéed vegetables and part of the Swiss cheese.

Pour into frypan and cover. Cook over low heat until set.

Bacon, Tomato and Cheese Stack-Ups

6	eggs	6
¼ cup	milk	50 mL
1 tbsp	finely chopped green onion	15 mL
¼ tsp	seasoned salt	1 mL
3 tbsp	butter	45 mL
8	slices side bacon, cooked	8
4	English muffins, split, toasted, buttered	4
8	slices tomato	8
8	slices process Canadian Cheddar cheese*	8

* Or you can use slices of Canadian Colby, Brick *or* Mozzarella cheese.

◄ In medium bowl, lightly beat eggs. Stir in milk, onion and salt.

◄ In large frypan, melt butter. Add egg mixture; cook and stir over low heat until eggs are cooked as desired.

◄ Cut each slice of bacon in half. Distribute bacon, tomato and egg mixture evenly among muffin halves. Cut Cheddar cheese slices in half diagonally and arrange over eggs. Broil until cheese is melted.

Makes 4 servings.
Preparation time: 5 minutes
Cooking time: 10 minutes

—TIP—

This easy "breakfast on a bun" tastes great made with cooked sausage patties or sliced cooked ham.

Quick and Creamy Scrambled Eggs

8	eggs	8
1	pkg (125 g) Cream cheese, cubed*	1
1/4 cup	milk	50 mL
1	green onion, sliced	1
1/2 tsp	salt	2 mL
	pinch ground black pepper	
1/4 cup	butter	50 mL

* Or you can use cubed Canadian Cheddar, Havarti *or* Gouda cheese.

◄ Place eggs and Cream cheese in blender container. Cover and blend at high speed until smooth. Add milk, onion, salt and pepper. Blend briefly until onion is coarsely chopped.

◄ In large frypan, melt butter. Add egg mixture; cook and stir over low heat until mixture is just set. Serve immediately.

Makes 4 or 5 servings.
Preparation time: 5 minutes
Cooking time: about 7 minutes

—TIP—

Be sure to refrigerate eggs to maintain freshness. Because the temperature of the refrigerator door fluctuates, it's better to keep the eggs inside the refrigerator. Store them in the carton to prevent moisture loss and odour absorption.

Banana French Toast

2 cups	milk	500 mL
4	eggs	4
1	medium ripe banana, peeled, sliced	1
2 tbsp	liquid honey	30 mL
¼ cup	frozen orange juice concentrate, thawed	50 mL
12	slices day-old whole wheat bread	12
	butter	
	sliced bananas	
	maple syrup	

◄ In blender container, combine milk, eggs, banana, honey and juice concentrate. Cover and blend at high speed until smooth. Pour over bread slices in large pan. Turn slices of bread over once; cover and refrigerate at least 3 hours, preferably overnight.

◄ In large frypan or electric skillet, melt a small amount of butter over medium heat. Cook bread until golden on both sides, adding more butter to pan as needed. Serve with sliced bananas and maple syrup.

Makes 6 servings.
Preparation time: 5 minutes
Standing time: 3 hours or overnight
Cooking time: 20 minutes

Cheddar Tomato Oven Omelet

8	slices side bacon, chopped	8
¼ cup	sliced green onions	50 mL
¾ cup	diced, seeded tomatoes	175 mL
1 tbsp	flour	15 mL
½ tsp	salt	2 mL
6	eggs	6
1 cup	milk	250 mL
1¼ cups	shredded Canadian Cheddar cheese, divided	300 mL
1 tbsp	grated Canadian Parmesan cheese	15 mL

◄ Preheat oven to 350°F (180°C).

◄ In large non-stick frypan, cook bacon until crisp. Drain, reserving 1 tbsp (15 mL) drippings; set bacon aside. Sauté onions in reserved drippings until tender; add tomatoes to pan. Sprinkle flour and salt over vegetables; toss lightly to coat.

◄ In large bowl, lightly beat eggs. Stir in milk. Add vegetable mixture, reserved bacon and 1 cup (250 mL) of the Cheddar cheese. Pour into greased 2-qt (2-L) shallow rectangular baking dish. Sprinkle with Parmesan cheese.

◄ Bake 25 minutes; remove from oven. Sprinkle remaining ¼ cup (50 mL) Cheddar cheese over omelet. Let stand 5 minutes and serve.

Makes 4 servings.
Preparation time: 15 minutes
Baking time: 25 minutes

Swiss Ham Oven Omelet: Substitute ¼ lb (125 g) cooked ham, cut into thin strips for bacon and 1 tbsp (15 mL) butter for bacon drippings. Use shredded Canadian Swiss *or* Gouda instead of Cheddar cheese.

VEGETABLES

Mushroom Stuffed Zucchini

3	medium zucchini	3
¼ cup	butter	50 mL
1 cup	chopped fresh mushrooms	250 mL
3 tbsp	chopped onion	45 mL
1	garlic clove, minced	1
1	egg, beaten	1
	pinch ground marjoram	
2/3 cup	shredded Canadian Cheddar cheese*, divided	150 mL
	salt and pepper	
¼ cup	fine dry bread crumbs	50 mL
1 tbsp	butter, melted	15 mL

* Or you can use shredded Canadian Mozzarella *or* Provolone cheese.

◄ Preheat oven to 350°F (180°C).

◄ In large saucepan, cook zucchini in boiling water 5 minutes; drain. Split zucchini lengthwise, scoop out pulp and chop. Reserve shells.

◄ In medium saucepan, melt ¼ cup (50 mL) butter. Sauté mushrooms, onions and garlic until tender and liquid has evaporated. Add zucchini pulp, cook and stir over low heat 5 minutes. Remove from heat and let cool slightly. Stir in egg, marjoram and half of the Cheddar cheese. Add salt and pepper to taste.

◄ Place zucchini shells in shallow baking dish. Divide mushroom-zucchini mixture evenly among shells.

◄ Combine bread crumbs and 1 tbsp (15 mL) melted butter. Sprinkle over filled shells. Top with remaining Cheddar cheese. Bake 30 minutes or until heated through.

Makes 6 servings.
Preparation time: 15 minutes
Baking time: 30 minutes

Cheesy Mashed Potatoes

6	all-purpose potatoes, peeled and quartered	6
½ cup	warm milk	125 mL
¼ cup	butter, softened	50 mL
1 cup	shredded Canadian Cheddar cheese*	250 mL
	salt and pepper	

* Or you can use crumbled Canadian Blue *or* chopped Brie cheese.

◄ In large saucepan, cook potatoes in boiling salted water 20 minutes or until tender; drain.

◄ Mash potatoes; add milk and butter. Stir in Cheddar cheese. Season with salt and pepper to taste and serve immediately.

Makes 4 or 5 servings.
Preparation time: 5 minutes
Cooking time: 20 minutes

—TIP—

Mashed potatoes should be free of lumps and a potato masher will do the job quickly and easily. If you like creamy smooth potatoes, whip them with a hand or electric beater, but do not use a blender or food processor or the potatoes will turn to glue.

Hot Stuffed Cheddar Potatoes

4	hot baked potatoes	4
1	can (10 oz/284 mL) cream of chicken soup	1
½ cup	milk	125 mL
2 cups	shredded Canadian Cheddar cheese	500 mL
1 cup	chopped cooked broccoli	250 mL
1 cup	chopped cooked chicken or turkey	250 mL
	salt and pepper	
	additional shredded Canadian Cheddar cheese	

◄ Preheat oven to 350°F (180°C).

◄ Cut potatoes in half lengthwise. Scoop out flesh into bowl leaving ¼-inch (5-mm) shells.

◄ In small saucepan, combine soup and milk; add Cheddar cheese. Cook and stir over low heat until cheese is melted; keep warm.

◄ Break up potato flesh; add broccoli and chicken. Stir in 1 cup (250 mL) of the cheese sauce. Add salt and pepper to taste.

◄ Spoon mixture into potato shells. Bake, covered, 15 minutes or until heated through. Pour remaining cheese sauce over each serving and top with more Cheddar cheese.

Makes 4 servings.
Preparation time: 20 minutes
Baking time: 15 minutes

Hot Stuffed Swiss Potatoes: Prepare potatoes as above. For the sauce, substitute cream of mushroom for chicken soup, Canadian Swiss for Cheddar cheese and chopped cooked ham for chicken.

— TIP —

To bake potatoes quickly in the microwave, scrub potatoes and pierce all over with a fork. Arrange in circle on microwave-safe plate. Microwave, uncovered, on HIGH (100%) 10 to 15 minutes; turn potatoes over once during cooking. Let potatoes stand, covered, 10 minutes before scooping out flesh.

Cheese-Topped Harvest Vegetable Bake

1/4 cup	butter	50 mL
2	medium onions, sliced	2
2	garlic cloves, minced	2
3 cups	*each* cubed eggplant and zucchini	750 mL
2 cups	quartered fresh mushrooms	500 mL
1	large green pepper, cut in 1/4-inch (5-mm) strips	1
2 cups	cubed tomatoes	500 mL
2 tbsp	chopped parsley	30 mL
1/2 tsp	*each* dried oregano and basil	2 mL
	salt and pepper	
1	pkg (200 g) Canadian Mozzarella cheese slices	1
2 tbsp	grated Canadian Parmesan cheese	30 mL

◄ Preheat oven to 400°F (200°C).

◄ In large saucepan, melt butter. Sauté onions and garlic until tender. Add eggplant, zucchini, mushrooms and green pepper to pan. Cook and stir over medium heat until vegetables are tender.

◄ Add tomatoes, parsley, oregano and basil. Bring to a boil over medium-high heat. Reduce heat and simmer, uncovered, 10 minutes. Add salt and pepper to taste.

◄ Spoon mixture into 1 1/2-qt (1.5-L) shallow rectangular casserole or four 1 1/2-cup (375-mL) shallow baking dishes. Slice Mozzarella cheese into strips and arrange in criss-cross pattern over vegetables. Sprinkle lightly with Parmesan cheese. Bake 10 minutes or until hot and bubbly.

Makes 4 servings.
Preparation time: 15 minutes
Baking time: 10 minutes

— TIP —

Choose eggplant with smooth skin and uniform colour. The eggplant should feel heavy for its size and should bounce back when pressed. Usually smaller eggplants are sweeter and more tender than larger ones.

Cheddar Corn Fritters

1 cup	fresh *or* frozen corn kernels	250 mL
1	egg, separated	1
1 tbsp	flour	15 mL
¼ tsp	salt	1 mL
	pinch ground black pepper	
1 cup	shredded 'old' Canadian Cheddar cheese*	250 mL
	butter	

* Or you can use shredded Canadian Mozzarella, Colby *or* Gouda cheese.

◄ In small saucepan, cook corn in small amount of boiling salted water 3 minutes or until tender-crisp; drain.

◄ In large bowl, combine corn, egg yolk, flour, salt and pepper. Add Cheddar cheese and toss to combine. In mixer bowl, beat egg white until stiff; fold in corn mixture.

◄ In large frypan, heat a small amount of butter over medium heat. Drop large spoonfuls of corn mixture into frypan. Cook until golden brown on both sides, adding more butter to pan as needed. Serve immediately.

Makes about 12 fritters.
Preparation time: 10 minutes
Cooking time: 10 minutes

Cauliflower en Casserole

1	large head cauliflower **and/or** broccoli, cut into florets	1
1/4 cup	butter	50 mL
2 cups	sliced fresh mushrooms	500 mL
1/3 cup	finely chopped celery	75 mL
2 tbsp	flour	30 mL
1/4 tsp	dry mustard	1 mL
1 1/4 cups	milk	300 mL
1 cup	shredded Canadian Swiss cheese*	250 mL
	salt and pepper	
1/2 cup	corn flake crumbs	125 mL
2 tbsp	butter, melted	30 mL

* Or you can use shredded Canadian Cheddar *or* Colby cheese.

◄ Preheat oven to 350°F (180°C).

◄ In large saucepan, cook cauliflower in boiling salted water until tender-crisp; drain.

◄ In medium saucepan, melt 1/4 cup (50 mL) butter. Sauté mushrooms and celery until tender and liquid has evaporated. Blend in flour and dry mustard. Gradually stir in milk. Cook and stir over medium heat until mixture boils and thickens.

◄ Remove from heat, add Swiss cheese and stir until cheese is melted. Season with salt and pepper to taste.

◄ Place cauliflower in 1 1/2-qt (1.5-L) shallow rectangular casserole; pour sauce over top. Combine crumbs and 2 tbsp (30 mL) melted butter; sprinkle over casserole. Bake 20 minutes or until heated through.

Makes 6 servings.
Preparation time: 15 minutes
Baking time: 20 minutes

Drain boiled potatoes and break up with fork.

Stir Cheddar cheese into potatoes.

Stir in sour cream, butter and green onions.

Au Gratin Potato Bake

6	medium potatoes, peeled, quartered	6
1 cup	shredded Canadian Cheddar cheese*	250 mL
3/4 cup	sour cream	175 mL
1/4 cup	butter, softened	50 mL
3 tbsp	finely chopped green onions	45 mL
	salt and pepper	
1 cup	fresh bread crumbs	250 mL
1 tbsp	butter, melted	15 mL

* Or you can use shredded Canadian Swiss, Mozzarella, Havarti *or* chopped Brie cheese.

◄ Preheat oven to 325°F (160°C).

◄ In large saucepan, cook potatoes in boiling salted water 20 minutes or until tender. Drain and break up with fork.

◄ Stir in Cheddar cheese, sour cream, 1/4 cup (50 mL) butter and green onions; add salt and pepper to taste.

◄ Place potato mixture in a 1 1/2-qt (1.5-L) shallow rectangular baking dish or four 1 1/2-cup (375-mL) shallow baking dishes. Combine bread crumbs and 1 tbsp (15 mL) melted butter; sprinkle over potatoes. Bake 15 minutes or until heated through.

Makes 4 to 6 servings.
Preparation time: 25 minutes
Baking time: 15 minutes

─ **TIP** ─

To make fresh bread crumbs, tear bread into chunks and place in blender container. Cover and blend thoroughly to make even crumbs. One slice equals about 1/2 cup (125 mL).

Honey Butter (top), Salt and Black Peppercorn Butter, Mexican Lime Coriander Butter

Honey Butter

½ cup	butter, softened	125 mL
⅓ cup	liquid honey	75 mL

◄ In small mixer bowl, beat together butter and honey. Spread liberally over hot cooked corn-on-the-cob.

Makes about ¾ cup (175 mL).
Preparation time: 5 minutes

Mexican Lime Coriander Butter

½ cup	butter, softened	125 mL
3 tbsp	lime juice	45 mL
2 tbsp	chopped fresh coriander	30 mL

◄ In small mixer bowl, beat together butter and lime juice; stir in coriander. Spread liberally over hot cooked corn-on-the-cob.

Makes about ⅔ cup (150 mL).
Preparation time: 5 minutes

Salt and Black Peppercorn Butter

½ cup	butter, softened	125 mL
1¼ tsp	salt	6 mL
	freshly cracked black peppercorns	

◄ In small bowl, beat together butter, salt and pepper to taste. Spread liberally over hot cooked corn-on-the-cob.

Makes about ½ cup (125 mL).
Preparation time: 5 minutes

Swiss Scalloped Potatoes

6 cups	thinly sliced new potatoes, divided	1.5 L
½ cup	finely chopped onion, divided	125 mL
2 cups	shredded Canadian Swiss cheese	500 mL
	salt and pepper	
1	can (10 oz/284 mL) chicken broth	1
1½ tbsp	flour	25 mL

◄ Preheat oven to 350°F (180°C).

◄ In 9-inch (23-cm) square baking dish, layer half the potato slices, half the onion then half the Swiss cheese; sprinkle lightly with salt and pepper. Repeat layering.

◄ Gradually stir chicken broth into flour until smooth. Pour over potatoes and cheese. Bake 1 hour or until potatoes are tender and cheese is golden brown. Let stand 5 minutes before serving.

Makes 6 servings.
Preparation time: 15 minutes
Baking time: 1 hour

Italian Scalloped Potatoes: Use shredded Canadian Mozzarella instead of Swiss cheese. Lightly sprinkle dried oregano *or* Italian seasoning over each layer of potatoes.

Zucchini, Corn and Tomatoes

2 lbs	zucchini	1 kg
¼ cup	butter	50 mL
½ cup	finely chopped onion	125 mL
½ tsp	dried oregano	2 mL
2	medium tomatoes, peeled, cut into eighths	2
1	can (12 oz/341 mL) kernel corn, drained	1
	salt and pepper	
⅔ cup	mayonnaise	150 mL
⅔ cup	grated Canadian Parmesan cheese	150 mL

◄ Slice zucchini into ½-inch (1-cm) thick diagonal slices; set aside.

◄ In large frypan, melt butter. Sauté onion until tender. Add zucchini and oregano. Cover and simmer 15 to 18 minutes or until zucchini is tender. Add tomatoes and corn; cook, uncovered, 5 minutes longer. Season with salt and pepper to taste.

◄ Place in shallow casserole. Combine mayonnaise and Parmesan cheese; spread over vegetables. Broil until lightly browned and serve.

Makes 6 to 8 servings.
Preparation time: 10 minutes
Cooking time: 25 minutes

— TIP —

To speed up the ripening of tomatoes place them in a brown paper bag for a day or two. If possible, do not store tomatoes in the refrigerator. The cold destroys their flavour. Instead, chill for 1 hour before serving.

Mushroom Buttered Green Beans

3 tbsp	butter	45 mL
1 cup	sliced fresh mushrooms	250 mL
1	pkg (300 g) frozen whole green beans	1
	salt and pepper	

◄ In medium saucepan, melt butter. Sauté mushrooms over medium-high heat until tender and liquid has evaporated. Reduce heat and add green beans.

◄ Cover and cook over medium heat, shaking pan frequently, until beans are tender-crisp. Remove lid and increase heat. Cook and stir until excess liquid has evaporated. Add salt and pepper to taste.

Makes 4 servings.
Preparation time: 5 minutes
Cooking time: 10 minutes

Mint Buttered Peas

¼ cup	butter	50 mL
½ tsp	dried mint leaves, crushed *or* fresh mint leaves, diced	2 mL
1	pkg (350 g) frozen baby peas	1
	salt and pepper	

◄ In medium saucepan, melt butter. Add mint and peas.

◄ Cover and cook over medium heat, shaking pan frequently, until peas are tender. Remove lid; increase heat. Cook and stir until any excess liquid has evaporated. Add salt and pepper to taste.

Makes 4 servings.
Preparation time: 5 minutes
Cooking time: 10 minutes

PASTA

Spaghetti Primavera

⅓ cup	butter	75 mL
1 cup	sliced fresh mushrooms	250 mL
½ cup	slivered green pepper	125 mL
¼ cup	chopped onion	50 mL
1	garlic clove, minced	1
1 cup	cooked broccoli florets	250 mL
1 cup	diced seeded tomato	250 mL
2 tbsp	chopped parsley	30 mL
¾ tsp	dried oregano	3 mL
6 oz	spaghetti *or* spaghettini	175 g
	salt and pepper	
	grated Canadian Parmesan cheese	

◄ In medium frypan, melt butter. Sauté mushrooms, green pepper, onion and garlic until tender. Add broccoli, tomato, parsley and oregano to pan; heat through, stirring occasionally.

◄ In large saucepan, cook spaghetti according to package directions; drain. Spoon vegetable mixture over spaghetti; toss well to coat. Add salt and pepper to taste. Sprinkle each serving with Parmesan cheese.

Makes 4 servings.
Preparation time: 15 minutes
Cooking time: 15 minutes

—TIP—

Here's a simple way to measure the spaghetti for this recipe: 6 oz (175 g) uncooked spaghetti equals a bunch about 1 inch (2.5 cm) in diameter.

Vegetable Lasagna Swirls

8	lasagna noodles	8
3 tbsp	butter	45 mL
4 cups	chopped fresh mushrooms	1 L
1 cup	chopped onion	250 mL
1	pkg (300 g) chopped frozen spinach, thawed, squeezed dry	1
2	eggs, beaten	2
2 cups	shredded Canadian Mozzarella cheese*	500 mL
1 cup	Cottage cheese**	250 mL
½ cup	grated Canadian Parmesan cheese	125 mL
	salt and pepper	
3	cans (7½ oz / 213 mL each) pizza sauce	3

* Or you can use shredded Canadian Provolone *or* Fontina cheese.

** Or you can use Canadian Ricotta cheese.

◄ Preheat oven to 350°F (180°C).

◄ In large saucepan or Dutch oven, cook lasagna according to package directions; drain.

◄ In large frypan, melt butter. Sauté mushrooms and onion until tender and liquid has evaporated; let cool. Stir in spinach, eggs, Mozzarella, Cottage and Parmesan cheeses. Add salt and pepper to taste.

◄ Spread about ¾ cup (175 mL) cheese mixture along each noodle, leaving 1 inch (2.5 cm) at one end uncovered. Roll up from filled end. Carefully cut rolls in half crosswise.

◄ Spread pizza sauce in 3-qt (3-L) rectangular baking dish. Arrange rolls, curly edges up, in sauce. Cover and bake 45 minutes or until heated through.

Makes 6 servings.
Preparation time: 25 minutes
Baking time: 45 minutes

Vegetable Lasagna: In shallow 3-qt (3-L) rectangular baking dish, alternately layer half of the lasagna noodles, half the vegetable-cheese mixture and half the sauce; repeat layers. Bake as above.

Fusilli Cheddar Bake

2 cups	fusilli pasta	500 mL
1 tbsp	butter, melted	15 mL
¼ cup	chopped green onions	50 mL
1	can (10 oz/284 mL) cream of mushroom soup	1
½ cup	milk	125 mL
2 cups	shredded Canadian Cheddar cheese	500 mL
1 cup	cooked peas	250 mL
1 cup	cooked, diced carrots	250 mL
	buttered bread cubes	

◄ Preheat oven to 350°F (180°C).

◄ In large saucepan, cook fusilli according to package directions; drain.

◄ In large saucepan, melt butter. Sauté onion until tender. Add soup. Gradually stir in milk. Add Cheddar cheese; cook and stir over low heat until cheese is melted. Stir in fusilli, peas and carrots.

◄ Spoon into 1½-qt (1.5-L) shallow rectangular casserole. Sprinkle with bread cubes. Bake 20 minutes or until heated through.

Makes 4 or 5 servings.
Preparation time: 20 minutes
Baking time: 20 minutes

Macaroni Mozzarella Bake: Substitute 1½ cups (375 mL) elbow macaroni for fusilli and use shredded Canadian Mozzarella instead of Cheddar cheese. Add ¼ cup (50 mL) grated Canadian Parmesan cheese. Substitute 1½ cups (375 mL) diced, seeded tomato and 1 tsp (5 mL) Italian seasoning for peas and carrots.

Linguini Milano

3 tbsp	butter	45 mL
¼ cup	chopped onion	50 mL
1	garlic clove, minced	1
2 tbsp	flour	30 mL
1 tsp	Italian seasoning	5 mL
1¾ cups	milk	425 mL
2 cups	shredded Canadian Mozzarella cheese*	500 mL
¼ cup	grated Canadian Parmesan cheese	50 mL
1 cup	slivered cooked ham	250 mL
1 cup	frozen peas, thawed	250 mL
	salt and pepper	
8 oz	linguini	250 g

* Or you can use shredded Canadian Cheddar, Colby *or* Provolone cheese.

◄ In medium saucepan, melt butter. Sauté onion and garlic until tender. Blend in flour and Italian seasoning. Gradually stir in milk. Cook and stir over medium heat until mixture boils and thickens. Remove from heat.

◄ Add Mozzarella and Parmesan cheeses and stir until cheeses are melted.

◄ Stir in ham and peas. Add salt and pepper to taste; keep warm.

◄ In large saucepan, cook linguini according to package directions; drain. Pour sauce over linguini. Toss well to coat and serve.

Makes 4 servings.
Preparation time: 10 minutes
Cooking time: 20 minutes

—TIP—

Use plenty of water to cook pasta (at least 1 qt/1 L for every 4 oz/125 g) so that the pasta moves freely and cooks evenly.

Pasta with Creamy Pesto Sauce

2 cups	packed fresh basil *or* parsley leaves	500 mL
3	garlic cloves, chopped	3
¼ cup	pine nuts *or* walnuts	50 mL
½ cup	grated Canadian Parmesan cheese	125 mL
2 tbsp	olive oil	30 mL
3 tbsp	butter	45 mL
⅓ cup	all-purpose flour	75 mL
3 cups	milk	750 mL
1 lb	pasta (spaghetti, fettucini *or* linguini)	500 g
	salt and pepper	
	additional grated Canadian Parmesan cheese	

◄ In blender container or food processor fitted with metal blade, combine basil, garlic and pine nuts. Cover and blend until finely chopped. Blend in Parmesan cheese and oil; set aside.

◄ In large saucepan, melt butter. Blend in flour. Gradually stir in milk. Cook and stir over medium heat until mixture boils and thickens. Blend in reserved pesto mixture; keep warm.

◄ In large saucepan, cook pasta according to package directions; drain. Pour sauce over pasta; toss well to coat. Add salt and pepper to taste. Cover and let stand 5 minutes before serving. Sprinkle each serving with more Parmesan cheese.

Makes 6 servings.
Preparation time: 10 minutes
Cooking time: 20 minutes

Variation: Fresh spinach can be used instead of basil *or* parsley in this recipe.

In food processor fitted with metal blade, combine basil, garlic and pine nuts. Cover and blend until finely chopped.

Blend in Parmesan cheese.

Blend in oil.

In large saucepan, melt butter and blend in flour.

Gradually stir in milk. Cook and stir over medium heat until mixture boils and thickens.

Blend in reserved pesto mixture.

Baked Manicotti

8	manicotti shells	8
½ lb	lean ground beef	250 g
½ cup	chopped onion	125 mL
1	garlic clove, minced	1
1	can (19 oz/540 mL) whole tomatoes	1
1	can (5½ oz/156 mL) tomato paste	1
1 tsp	sugar	5 mL
½ tsp	*each* dried basil and oregano	2 mL
	salt and pepper	
1½ cups	shredded Canadian Mozzarella cheese*	375 mL
1 cup	Cottage cheese**	250 mL
½ cup	grated Canadian Parmesan cheese	125 mL
2	eggs, beaten	2
1 tbsp	chopped parsley	15 mL
1 tsp	salt	5 mL

◄ Preheat oven to 350°F (180°C).

◄ In large saucepan or Dutch oven, cook manicotti according to package directions; drain.

◄ In large frypan, sauté beef, onion and garlic until meat is browned and vegetables are tender; drain. Add tomatoes, tomato paste, sugar, basil and oregano. Bring to a boil over medium-high heat. Reduce heat, cover and simmer 30 minutes. Add salt and pepper to taste.

◄ In large bowl, combine Mozzarella, Cottage and Parmesan cheeses, eggs, parsley and 1 tsp (5 mL) salt.

◄ Place half of the tomato sauce mixture in 2-qt (2-L) shallow rectangular baking dish. Set remaining sauce aside and keep warm. Divide cheese mixture among manicotti shells; arrange in dish. Bake, uncovered, 30 minutes or until heated through. Pour reserved sauce over manicotti and serve.

Makes 4 servings.
Preparation time: 45 minutes
Baking time: 30 minutes

* Or you can use shredded Canadian Provolone *or* Fontina cheese.

** Or you can use Canadian Ricotta cheese.

Macaroni 'n' Three Cheeses

2 cups	elbow macaroni	500 mL
5 tbsp	butter, divided	75 mL
¼ cup	chopped green onions	50 mL
¼ cup	all-purpose flour	50 mL
½ tsp	dry mustard	2 mL
2 cups	milk	500 mL
1½ cups	shredded Canadian Cheddar cheese	375 mL
1 cup	shredded Canadian Swiss cheese	250 mL
1 cup	shredded Canadian Brick cheese (with or without caraway seeds)	250 mL
1 tbsp	chopped parsley	15 mL
	salt and pepper	
1 cup	fresh bread crumbs	250 mL

◄ Preheat oven to 350°F (180°C).

◄ In large saucepan, cook macaroni according to package directions; drain.

◄ In large saucepan, melt 4 tbsp (60 mL) of the butter. Sauté onion until tender. Blend in flour and dry mustard. Gradually stir in milk. Cook and stir over medium heat until mixture boils and thickens. Remove from heat.

◄ Add Cheddar, Swiss and Brick cheeses and stir until cheeses are melted. (Return to low heat if necessary to melt all of the cheese.)

◄ Fold in macaroni and parsley. Add salt and pepper to taste. Spoon mixture into 2-qt (2-L) shallow rectangular casserole.

◄ Melt remaining 1 tbsp (15 mL) butter; toss with bread crumbs. Sprinkle over casserole. Bake 20 minutes or until heated through.

Makes 6 servings.
Preparation time: 30 minutes
Baking time: 20 minutes

Cheesy Buttons and Bows

1½ cups	bowtie-shaped pasta	375 mL
2 tbsp	butter	30 mL
2 tbsp	flour	30 mL
½ tsp	chicken bouillon mix	2 mL
1 cup	milk	250 mL
1½ cups	shredded Canadian Colby cheese*	375 mL
4	wieners, cut in ¼-inch (5-mm) slices	4
¾ cup	frozen peas, thawed	175 mL
1-2 tbsp	ketchup	15-30 mL
	toast cut-outs	

* Or you can use shredded Canadian Cheddar *or* Marble cheese.

◄ In large saucepan, cook pasta according to package directions; drain.

◄ In large saucepan, melt butter. Blend in flour and bouillon mix. Gradually stir in milk. Cook and stir over medium heat until mixture boils and thickens. Remove from heat.

◄ Add Colby cheese and stir until cheese is melted. Add pasta, wieners, peas and ketchup. Cook and stir over low heat until heated through; do not let mixture boil. Serve with toast cut-outs.

Makes 4 servings.
Preparation time: 15 minutes
Cooking time: 15 minutes

Variation: Substitute wagon wheel-shaped pasta for bowtie-shaped pasta. To make toast cut-outs, use cookie cutters (hearts, stars, teddy bears, etc.) to cut fun shapes from buttered toast.

Sauté beef and green pepper until meat is browned; drain. Stir in tomato sauce and oregano.

In small bowl, combine Cottage cheese, half of the Cheddar cheese, sour cream, green onions and salt.

Layer half of the noodles in ungreased 8-inch (20-cm) square baking dish.

Dairy Delicious Casserole

3 cups	medium noodles	750 mL
1 lb	lean ground beef	500 g
½ cup	chopped green pepper	125 mL
1	can (14 oz/398 mL) tomato sauce	1
½ tsp	dried oregano	2 mL
1 cup	Cottage cheese*	250 mL
1 cup	shredded Canadian Cheddar cheese**, divided	250 mL
¼ cup	sour cream	50 mL
2 tbsp	finely chopped green onions	30 mL
½ tsp	salt	2 mL

* Or you can use Canadian Ricotta cheese.

** Or you can use shredded Canadian Mozzarella *or* Havarti cheese.

◄ Preheat oven to 350°F (180°C).

◄ In large saucepan, cook noodles according to package directions; drain.

◄ In large frypan, sauté beef and green pepper until meat is browned and green pepper is tender; drain. Stir in tomato sauce and oregano. Over medium heat, bring mixture to a boil, stirring constantly. Remove from heat and set aside.

◄ In small bowl, combine Cottage cheese, half of the Cheddar cheese, sour cream, green onions and salt. Layer half of the noodles in ungreased 8-inch (20-cm) square baking dish. Cover with cheese mixture. Layer remaining noodles and top with meat sauce. Sprinkle remaining ½ cup (125 mL) Cheddar cheese over meat sauce.

◄ Bake, uncovered, for 30 minutes or until heated through. Let stand 5 minutes before serving.

Makes 4 to 6 servings.
Preparation time: 15 minutes
Baking time: 30 minutes

Cover noodles with cheese mixture.

Layer remaining noodles and top with meat sauce.

Sprinkle remaining Cheddar cheese over meat sauce.

Jumbo Shells Italiano

16	jumbo pasta shells	16
1½ cups	shredded Canadian Mozzarella cheese*	375 mL
1 cup	Cottage cheese**	250 mL
½ cup	grated Canadian Parmesan cheese	125 mL
2	eggs, beaten	2
1 tbsp	chopped parsley	15 mL
1	can (14 oz/398 mL) Italian tomato sauce	1

* Or you can use shredded Canadian Provolone, Cheddar *or* Gouda cheese.

** Or you can use Canadian Ricotta cheese.

◄ Preheat oven to 350°F (180°C).

◄ In large saucepan, cook shells according to package directions; drain.

◄ In medium bowl, combine Mozzarella, Cottage and Parmesan cheeses, eggs and parsley. Fill each shell with cheese mixture.

◄ Divide tomato sauce among 4 individual shallow casseroles. Arrange 4 filled shells in each casserole. Cover and bake 20 minutes or until heated through.

Makes 4 servings.
Preparation time: 30 minutes
Baking time: 20 minutes

—TIP—

If you don't want to use individual casseroles, spread tomato sauce in 2-qt (2-L) shallow rectangular casserole; arrange filled shells on top. Cover and increase baking time to 30 minutes.

FISH

Baked Sole Roll-Ups

1½ lbs	sole fillets (thawed if frozen)	750 g
2 tbsp	lemon juice	30 mL
2 tbsp	butter	30 mL
2 tbsp	flour	30 mL
1 tsp	chicken bouillon mix	5 mL
½ tsp	dry mustard	2 mL
1½ cups	milk	375 mL
½ cup	shredded Canadian Swiss cheese*	125 mL
2 tbsp	grated Canadian Parmesan cheese*	30 mL
	salt and pepper	

* Or you can use ¾ cup (175 mL) shredded Canadian Cheddar instead of both Swiss and Parmesan cheeses.

◄ Preheat oven to 400°F (200°C).

◄ If fillets are large, cut lengthwise in half. Roll up fish and secure with toothpicks if necessary. Place in shallow rectangular baking dish and sprinkle with lemon juice. Cover with foil. Bake 14 minutes or until fish flakes with fork.

◄ In medium saucepan, melt butter. Blend in flour, bouillon mix and dry mustard. Gradually stir in milk. Cook and stir over medium heat until mixture boils and thickens. Remove from heat.

◄ Add Swiss and Parmesan cheeses and stir until cheeses are melted. Add salt and pepper to taste. Drain fish rolls and serve with cheese sauce.

Makes 4 servings.
Preparation time: 10 minutes
Baking time: 14 minutes

Swiss Salmon Mornay

2 tbsp	butter	30 mL
2 tbsp	flour	30 mL
2 tsp	chicken bouillon mix	10 mL
½ tsp	dry mustard	2 mL
1¾ cups	milk	425 mL
¾ cup	shredded Canadian Swiss cheese	175 mL
2	cans (7½ oz/213 g *each*) salmon, drained, in chunks, skin removed	2
2 cups	cooked broccoli florets	500 mL

◄ Preheat oven to 350°F (180°C).

◄ In medium saucepan, melt butter. Blend in flour, bouillon mix and mustard. Gradually stir in milk. Cook and stir over medium heat until mixture boils and thickens. Remove from heat.

◄ Add Swiss cheese and stir until cheese is melted. Fold in salmon.

◄ Divide mixture among 4 small shallow casseroles. Arrange broccoli around outside edges. Bake 20 minutes or until heated through.

Makes 4 servings.
Preparation time: 15 minutes
Baking time: 20 minutes

Cheddar Fish Casseroles: Reduce dry mustard to ¼ tsp (1 mL) and milk to 1½ cups (375 mL). Use shredded Canadian Cheddar instead of Swiss cheese and 2 cups (500 mL) cooked, chunked cod, halibut *or* sole instead of salmon. Substitute 3 cups (750 mL) cooked rice tossed with 3 tbsp (45 mL) chopped parsley for broccoli. Place rice on bottom of casseroles.

Broiled Teriyaki Buttered Fish

¼ cup	butter, melted	50 mL
1½ tbsp	bottled teriyaki sauce	25 mL
1½ tbsp	chopped green onions	25 mL
1	garlic clove, minced	1
1½ lbs	thin fish fillets (thawed if frozen)	750 g

◄ In small bowl, combine butter, teriyaki sauce, onion and garlic; stir well.

◄ Cut fish into 1-inch (2.5-cm) wide strips. Thread strips, accordion-style, onto metal or wooden skewers*.

◄ Brush fish with butter baste. Broil, basting and turning once or twice, until fish flakes with fork.

* If using wooden skewers, soak them in water for 30 minutes prior to broiling to prevent them from burning.

Makes 6 servings.
Preparation time: 15 minutes
Cooking time: 8 minutes

Cream butter and gradually beat in lemon juice. Add herbs and salt and pepper to taste.

Place butter mixture on a sheet of plastic wrap and shape into a roll about 1 1/2 inches (4 cm) in diameter.

Seal ends well and refrigerate at least 2 hours. To serve, slice with knife dipped in hot water.

Savoury Buttered Fish

1	small cucumber, thinly sliced	1
1 lb	white fish fillets* (thawed if frozen)	500 g
	lemon juice	
	salt	
	Tomato Chive Butter, Herb Butter *or* Lemon Parsley Butter	

◄ Preheat oven to 450°F (230°C).

◄ Place overlapping cucumber slices in centre of a large piece of foil shiny side up. Pat fish dry and arrange in single layer on top of cucumber. Sprinkle with lemon juice and salt. Bring edges of foil together; fold to seal. Place on baking sheet.

◄ Bake 10 minutes or until fish flakes with fork. Drain fish and cucumber. Serve with Tomato Chive Butter, Herb Butter or Lemon Parsley Butter.

* You can use haddock, halibut, bluefish, cod *or* any other kind of white fish fillets for this recipe.

Makes 4 servings
Preparation time: 10 minutes
Baking time: 10 minutes

Tomato Chive Butter: Cream 1/2 cup (125 mL) softened butter. Gradually beat in 1 tbsp (15 mL) tomato paste, 1 tbsp (15 mL) dried chives and 1 tsp (5 mL) lemon juice. Add salt and pepper to taste. *Makes about 1/2 cup (125 mL).*

Herb Butter: Cream 1/2 cup (125 mL) softened butter. Gradually beat in 2 tbsp (30 mL) lemon juice and 1 tsp (5 mL) dried tarragon, dill, basil *or* oregano. Add salt and pepper to taste. *Makes about 1/2 cup (125 mL).*

Lemon Parsley Butter: Cream 1/2 cup (125 mL) softened butter. Gradually beat in 1 1/2 tbsp (25 mL) *each* lemon juice and chopped parsley. Add salt and pepper to taste. *Makes about 1/2 cup (125 mL).*

Baked Fish au Gratin

1	pkg (400 g) frozen cod, haddock *or* sole fillets	1
2 tbsp	butter, divided	30 mL
2 tsp	lemon juice	10 mL
	salt and paprika	
	hot cooked noodles *or* rice	
1 tbsp	flour	15 mL
1/4 tsp	dry mustard	1 mL
3/4 cup	milk	175 mL
1 cup	shredded Canadian Cheddar cheese*	250 mL
1 tbsp	chopped parsley	15 mL
	salt and pepper	

* Or you can use shredded Canadian Colby *or* Gouda cheese.

◄ Preheat oven to 450°F (220°C).

◄ Cut frozen fish crosswise into 4 pieces. Place fillets on large piece of foil shiny side up. Dot fish with 1 tbsp (15 mL) of butter. Sprinkle with lemon juice, salt and paprika. Bring edges of foil together; fold to seal. Place on baking sheet. Bake 30 minutes or until fish flakes with fork.

◄ Drain fish, reserving 1/3 cup (75 mL) liquid in foil. Arrange cooked fish on noodles; keep warm.

◄ In medium saucepan, melt remaining 1 tbsp (15 mL) butter. Blend in flour and mustard. Gradually stir in milk and reserved fish liquid. Cook and stir over medium heat until mixture boils and thickens. Remove from heat.

◄ Add Cheddar cheese and stir until cheese is melted. Add parsley and salt and pepper to taste. To serve, pour sauce over fish and noodles.

Makes 4 servings.
Preparation time: 20 minutes
Baking time: 30 minutes

Tuna Casserole Deluxe

2 cups	broad egg noodles	500 mL
1/4 cup	butter	50 mL
1/2 cup	finely chopped onion	125 mL
1/4 cup	all-purpose flour	50 mL
3/4 tsp	dried basil	3 mL
3 cups	milk	750 mL
1/4 cup	grated Canadian Parmesan cheese	50 mL
2 cups	chopped cooked broccoli	500 mL
2	cans (6.5 oz / 184 g *each*) solid tuna, drained, flaked	2
	salt and pepper	
1/3 cup	fine dry bread crumbs	75 mL
2 tbsp	butter, melted	30 mL

◄ In large saucepan, cook noodles according to package directions; drain.

◄ Preheat oven to 350°F (180°C).

◄ In medium saucepan, melt 1/4 cup (50 mL) butter. Sauté onion until tender. Blend in flour and basil. Gradually stir in milk. Cook and stir over medium heat until mixture boils and thickens. Remove from heat; add Parmesan cheese and stir until cheese is melted.

◄ Fold in noodles, broccoli and tuna; add salt and pepper to taste. Turn into 1 1/2-qt (1.5-L) shallow rectangular casserole.

◄ Combine bread crumbs and 2 tbsp (30 mL) butter. Sprinkle around outside edge of casserole. Bake 20 minutes or until heated through.

Makes 4 servings.
Preparation time: 25 minutes
Baking time: 20 minutes

Fish Baked in Foil Packets

2 tbsp	butter	30 mL
2 tbsp	sliced green onions	30 mL
2 cups	thinly sliced fresh mushrooms	500 mL
1 cup	thinly sliced carrots	250 mL
1 cup	thinly sliced celery	250 mL
	seasoned salt	
1 lb	fish fillets (thawed if frozen)	500 g
4 tsp	lemon juice, divided	20 mL

◄ Preheat oven to 350°F (180°C).

◄ In large frypan, melt butter. Sauté onions, mushrooms, carrots and celery until vegetables are tender-crisp and liquid has evaporated; add salt to taste.

◄ Cut aluminum foil into four 12-inch (30-cm) squares; place shiny side up. Distribute vegetable mixture over centre of each square; top with fish. Sprinkle 1 tsp (5 mL) lemon juice over each serving. Fold half of foil over to form triangle and seal edges.

◄ Place packages on shallow baking sheet. Bake 15 minutes or until fish flakes with fork. To serve in foil, cut "X" opening with scissors in top of each package.

Makes 4 servings.
Preparation time: 15 minutes
Baking time: 15 minutes

Sauté onions, mushrooms, carrots and celery until vegetables are tender-crisp.

Distribute vegetable mixture over centre of each foil square.

Place fish over vegetables and sprinkle with lemon juice.

Salmon Loaf with Dilly Cucumber Sauce

2	cans (7½ oz / 213 g *each*) salmon, drained, flaked	2
¾ cup	fine dry bread crumbs	175 mL
⅔ cup	milk	150 mL
2	eggs	2
½ cup	*each* finely chopped green pepper and onion	125 mL
¼ cup	*each* finely chopped celery and pimento	50 mL
¼ tsp	salt	1 mL
	pinch ground black pepper	

Dilly Cucumber Sauce:

2 tbsp	butter	30 mL
½ cup	well-drained shredded seedless cucumber	125 mL
¼ cup	chopped onion	50 mL
2 tbsp	flour	30 mL
½ tsp	dried dill weed	2 mL
1¼ cups	milk	300 mL
2 tbsp	lemon juice	30 mL
	salt and pepper	

◄ Preheat oven to 350°F (180°C).

◄ In large bowl, combine salmon, bread crumbs, milk, eggs, green pepper, onion, celery, pimento, salt and pepper; mix thoroughly.

◄ Pack mixture into greased 8½ x 4½-inch (21 x 11-cm) loaf pan. Bake 40 minutes or until set.

◄ Meanwhile, prepare Dilly Cucumber Sauce: In medium saucepan, melt butter. Sauté cucumber and chopped onion until tender. Blend in flour and dill weed. Gradually stir in milk. Cook and stir over medium heat until mixture boils and thickens. Stir in lemon juice; add salt and pepper to taste.

◄ When loaf is set, remove from oven and loosen edges with knife. Turn out onto platter. Slice and serve with Dilly Cucumber Sauce.

Makes 6 servings.
Preparation time: 15 minutes
Baking time: 40 minutes

POULTRY

Lemon Butter-Glazed Chicken

4	boneless skinless chicken breast halves	4
	flour	
3 tbsp	butter	45 mL
3 tbsp	water	45 mL
1 tbsp	lemon juice	15 mL
1½ tsp	chicken bouillon mix	7 mL
	chopped parsley	
	lemon slices	

◄ Pound chicken lightly to flatten; coat with flour and shake to remove excess.

◄ In large frypan, melt butter. Add chicken breasts and sauté until golden brown on both sides. Add water, lemon juice and chicken bouillon mix to pan; stir until dissolved. Bring to a boil over medium-high heat. Reduce heat, cover and simmer 5 minutes or until chicken is no longer pink in centre. Remove chicken from pan; keep warm.

◄ Cook and stir pan juices over high heat until thickened and syrupy, 1 to 2 minutes. Pour glaze over chicken, sprinkle with parsley and garnish with lemon slices.

Makes 4 servings.
Preparation time: 10 minutes
Cooking time: 15 minutes

—TIP—

Be sure to wash all preparation surfaces and utensils thoroughly with hot soapy water after contact with raw poultry.

Hearty Chicken and Vegetable Stew

2 tbsp	butter	30 mL
3½ lbs	chicken pieces	1.75 kg
3 cups	water	750 mL
1 cup	finely chopped onion	250 mL
2 tbsp	chicken bouillon mix	30 mL
2 tsp	poultry seasoning	10 mL
8	small carrots, cut in 1-inch (2.5-cm) pieces	8
6	small potatoes, quartered	6
3	stalks celery, cut in 1-inch (2.5-cm) pieces	3
1½ cups	frozen peas	375 mL
1¾ cups	milk	425 mL
¼ cup	all-purpose flour	50 mL
	salt and pepper	

◄ In large saucepan, melt butter. Sauté chicken until golden brown on both sides; drain. Stir in water, onion, chicken bouillon mix and poultry seasoning. Bring to a boil over medium-high heat. Reduce heat, cover and simmer 15 minutes.

◄ Add carrots, potatoes and celery. Simmer, covered, 20 minutes longer or until chicken and vegetables are cooked. Add peas and cook 3 to 5 minutes longer.

◄ Gradually stir milk into flour until smoothly combined. Add to pan. Cook and stir over medium heat until mixture boils and thickens. Season with salt and pepper to taste.

Makes 6 servings.
Preparation time: 10 minutes
Cooking time: 45 minutes

— TIP —

It's important to cook chicken thoroughly. To test pieces with bones, insert a fork into the chicken. If the meat is tender and juices run clear, the chicken is done. For boneless chicken, check that the meat is no longer pink in the centre.

Parmesan Dijon Chicken

2 tbsp	hot pepper sauce, divided	30 mL
2 tbsp	butter, melted	30 mL
¾ cup	fresh bread crumbs	175 mL
¾ cup	grated Canadian Parmesan cheese	175 mL
⅓ cup	Dijon mustard	75 mL
1 tbsp	water	15 mL
8	boneless skinless chicken breast halves	8
	Spicy Sauce (optional)	

◄ Preheat oven to 450°F (230°C).

◄ In small bowl, combine 1 tbsp (15 mL) of the hot pepper sauce and butter. Toss mixture with bread crumbs and Parmesan cheese; set aside.

◄ In shallow dish, combine mustard with remaining 1 tbsp (15 mL) hot pepper sauce and water. Coat chicken with mustard mixture; place on greased 15 x 10-inch (38 x 25-cm) shallow baking pan.

◄ Spoon Parmesan cheese mixture over chicken and press down lightly. Bake 20 minutes or until chicken is no longer pink in centre. Serve with Spicy Sauce, if desired.

Makes 8 servings.
Preparation time: 10 minutes
Baking time: 20 minutes

Spicy Sauce: In small saucepan, combine ⅓ cup (75 mL) hot pepper sauce, 2 tbsp (30 mL) butter and 2 tsp (10 mL) lemon juice. Heat until butter is melted. *Makes about ½ cup (125 mL).*

Turkey and Wild Rice Casserole

1	pkg (170 g) long grain and wild rice	1
1 cup	thinly sliced celery	250 mL
2 cups	cubed cooked turkey *or* chicken	500 mL
2	pkgs (300 g *each*) broccoli spears, cooked, drained	2
2 tbsp	butter	30 mL
2 tbsp	flour	30 mL
2 tsp	chicken bouillon mix	10 mL
½ tsp	dry mustard	2 mL
1¾ cups	milk	425 mL
2 cups	shredded Canadian Swiss cheese	500 mL
2 tbsp	grated Canadian Parmesan cheese	30 mL
	salt and pepper	

◄ Preheat oven 350°F (180°C).

◄ In medium saucepan, prepare rice according to package directions; stir in celery. Alternately layer cooked rice and turkey into 2-qt (2-L) round casserole. Arrange broccoli spears on top.

◄ In small saucepan, melt butter. Blend in flour, bouillon mix and dry mustard. Gradually stir in milk. Cook and stir over medium heat until mixture boils and thickens. Remove from heat.

◄ Add Swiss and Parmesan cheeses and stir until cheeses are melted. Add salt and pepper to taste.

◄ Pour over broccoli and rice. Bake, uncovered, 35 minutes or until heated through.

Makes 5 or 6 servings.
Preparation time: 20 minutes
Baking time: 35 minutes

Turkey Breast Parmigiana

½ cup	grated Canadian Parmesan cheese	125 mL
½ cup	fine dry bread crumbs	125 mL
2 lbs	boneless skinless turkey breast, cut in 8 pieces	1 kg
⅓ cup	all-purpose flour	75 mL
2	eggs, lightly beaten	2
	butter	
3 cups	spaghetti *or* pizza sauce, divided	750 mL
2	pkgs (200 g *each*) Canadian Mozzarella cheese* slices	2

* Or you can use thinly sliced Canadian Provolone cheese.

◄ In shallow dish, combine Parmesan cheese and bread crumbs. Pound turkey lightly to flatten. Dip pieces into flour, then eggs and finally cheese mixture. Shake lightly to remove excess. Let pieces stand on wire rack 10 minutes.

◄ Preheat oven to 350°F (180°C).

◄ In large frypan, melt a little butter. Sauté turkey until golden on both sides, adding more butter to pan as needed.

◄ Spread half the spaghetti sauce on the bottom of 3-qt (3-L) shallow rectangular baking dish. Alternately layer turkey and Mozzarella cheese. Spoon remaining sauce around edges of dish.

◄ Bake, uncovered, 25 minutes or until heated through.

Makes 8 servings.
Preparation time: 25 minutes
Baking time: 25 minutes

Dip turkey pieces into flour, then eggs and finally into cheese mixture. Shake lightly to remove excess.

Sauté turkey until golden on both sides, adding more butter to pan as needed.

Spread half the spaghetti sauce in shallow rectangular baking dish. Alternately layer turkey and Mozzarella cheese.

Chicken Patties Paprika

1½ lbs	ground chicken *or* turkey	750 g
1½ cups	milk, divided	375 mL
⅔ cup	fine dry bread crumbs	150 mL
1 tsp	garlic salt	5 mL
1	egg	1
	butter	
1 cup	chopped onion	250 mL
1 tbsp	paprika	15 mL
2 tsp	chicken bouillon mix	10 mL
½ cup	water	125 mL
1 tbsp	flour	15 mL
½ cup	sour cream	125 mL
	salt and pepper	

◄ In large bowl, combine chicken, ½ cup (125 mL) of the milk, bread crumbs, garlic salt and egg. Mix well and shape into 6 patties.

◄ In large frypan, melt a little butter. Sauté patties on both sides until golden, adding more butter to pan as needed. Remove patties and set aside.

◄ Melt a little more butter in same frypan; sauté onion until tender. Blend in paprika and bouillon mix; stir in water. Return patties to pan. Bring mixture to a boil over medium-high heat. Reduce heat, cover and simmer 10 minutes or until patties are cooked. Remove patties from pan and keep warm.

◄ Gradually stir remaining 1 cup (250 mL) milk into flour until smooth; add to pan. Cook and stir over medium heat until mixture boils and thickens. Remove from heat and stir in sour cream. Season with salt and pepper to taste. Pour sauce over patties and serve.

Makes 6 servings.
Preparation time: 20 minutes
Cooking time: 25 minutes

—TIP—

Paprika is a common seasoning in Hungarian dishes. You can either use the mild supermarket variety, or for spicier patties, use hot Hungarian paprika, available at specialty stores.

Oven Fried Chicken

¼ cup	all-purpose flour	50 mL
1½ tsp	*each* salt, curry powder and poultry seasoning	7 mL
1 tsp	paprika	5 mL
¼ tsp	ground black pepper	1 mL
3 lbs	chicken pieces	1.5 kg
⅓ cup	butter, melted	75 mL

◄ Preheat oven to 450°F (230°C).

◄ In large plastic zipper bag, combine flour, salt, curry powder, poultry seasoning, paprika and pepper. Shake 2 or 3 chicken pieces at a time in seasoned flour. Place butter in 2-qt (2-L) shallow rectangular baking dish. Place chicken pieces in dish, skin side down.

◄ Bake 20 minutes. Turn chicken over and bake 15 minutes longer or until juices run clear when pierced with fork.

Makes 4 servings.
Preparation time: 10 minutes
Baking time: 35 minutes

— TIP —

You can store fresh or cooked chicken for up to two days; cover or wrap tightly in plastic and refrigerate.

Chicken Breast Suprême

	butter	
8	boneless skinless chicken breast halves	8
½ cup	finely chopped onion	125 mL
¾ tsp	poultry seasoning *or* ground thyme	3 mL
1	chicken bouillon cube	1
½ cup	boiling water	125 mL
1 cup	light *or* table cream	250 mL
1 tbsp	flour	15 mL
¼ cup	toasted sliced almonds	50 mL
	salt and pepper	

◄ In large frypan, melt a little butter. Sauté chicken until golden brown on both sides, adding more butter to pan as needed. Remove from pan.

◄ In same pan, sauté onion until tender. Return chicken to pan. Sprinkle with poultry seasoning or thyme. Dissolve bouillon cube in boiling water and pour over chicken. Bring to a boil over medium-high heat. Reduce heat, cover and simmer 20 minutes or until chicken is no longer pink in centre. Remove chicken and keep warm.

◄ Gradually stir cream into flour until smooth; add to pan along with almonds. Cook and stir over medium heat until mixture boils and thickens. Add salt and pepper to taste. Pour sauce over chicken and serve.

Makes 8 servings.
Preparation time: 10 minutes
Cooking time: 40 to 45 minutes

Add chicken to soy sauce mixture and toss to coat.

Add chicken to butter in frypan and stir-fry 2 minutes or until chicken is cooked.

In same pan, melt remaining butter. Add carrot and onion and stir-fry 3 minutes.

Chicken and Vegetable Stir-Fry

1 lb	boneless skinless chicken breasts	500 g
3 tbsp	soy sauce, divided	45 mL
3 tbsp	corn starch, divided	45 mL
1 tsp	grated fresh ginger root (optional)	5 mL
1 tsp	sugar	5 mL
1-2	garlic cloves, minced	1-2
¼ tsp	crushed red chilies	1 mL
1½ cups	water	375 mL
5 tbsp	butter, divided	75 mL
2 cups	thinly sliced carrots	500 mL
1	onion, diced large	1
1	*each* red and green pepper, cut in ¼-inch (5-mm) strips, halved	1
	hot cooked rice	

◄ Cut chicken into thin narrow strips.

◄ In medium bowl, combine 2 tbsp (30 mL) of the soy sauce, 1 tbsp (15 mL) of the corn starch, ginger if desired, sugar and garlic. Add chicken and toss to coat; set aside.

◄ Blend crushed chilies with remaining corn starch and soy sauce. Stir in water and set aside.

◄ In large frypan, melt 3 tbsp (45 mL) of the butter over high heat. Add chicken and stir-fry 2 minutes or until chicken is cooked; remove from pan.

◄ Melt remaining 2 tbsp (30 mL) butter in same pan over high heat. Add carrot and onion; stir-fry 3 minutes. Add peppers; stir-fry 2 minutes. Stir in chicken and soy sauce mixture. Cook and stir over medium heat until sauce boils and thickens. Serve with rice.

Makes 4 servings.
Preparation time: 15 minutes
Cooking time: 15 minutes

Add peppers; stir-fry 2 minutes.

Stir chicken into stir-fried vegetables.

Add soy sauce mixture. Cook and stir over medium heat until sauce boils and thickens.

MEAT

Apple Cream Pork Chops

4	lean pork chops, about 3/4-inch (2-cm) thick	4
	flour	
	butter	
1/3 cup	finely chopped onion	75 mL
1 tsp	beef bouillon mix	5 mL
	pinch ground thyme	
1/2 cup	apple juice	125 mL
6	thick slices red apple	6
2/3 cup	whipping cream	150 mL
	salt and pepper	

◄ Coat meat with flour; shake lightly to remove excess.

◄ In large frypan, melt a little butter. Add meat and sauté until golden brown on both sides. Remove from pan and set aside.

◄ Sauté onion in same pan until tender, adding more butter if necessary. Blend in bouillon mix and thyme; stir in apple juice. Return meat to pan. Bring to a boil over medium-high heat. Reduce heat, cover and simmer 50 minutes or until meat is tender.

◄ Arrange apple slices over meat 15 minutes before end of cooking time. When done, remove meat and apples from pan; keep warm.

◄ Stir cream into pan juices; bring to a boil. Cook and stir over medium heat until sauce is reduced to desired thickness. Add salt and pepper to taste. Pour sauce over meat and apples; serve.

Makes 4 servings.
Preparation time: 10 minutes
Cooking time: 70 minutes

Mexicana Cheeseburgers

1 lb	lean ground beef	500 g
1	pkg (about 35 g) taco seasoning mix	1
1	egg, beaten	1
4 oz	Canadian Colby cheese*, sliced	125 g
	leaf lettuce and sliced tomatoes	
	hamburger buns, split, toasted	
	bottled taco sauce (optional)	

* Or you can use sliced Canadian Monterey Jack *or* Brick cheese.

◄ In large bowl, combine beef, seasoning mix and egg; mix well. Shape into 4 patties. Barbecue or broil until cooked as desired. Top with Colby cheese; cook until cheese is melted.

◄ To serve, place lettuce and tomato slices on bottom halves of buns. Top with meat patties, taco sauce if desired, and tops of buns.

Makes 4 servings.
Preparation time: 10 minutes
Cooking time: 4 to 8 minutes per side

Italiano Cheeseburgers: In medium frypan, melt 2 tbsp (30 mL) butter. Sauté 3 cups (750 mL) sliced fresh mushrooms until tender and liquid has evaporated; keep warm. Use 1/2 cup (125 mL) grated Canadian Parmesan cheese, 3/4 tsp (3 mL) Italian seasoning and pinch garlic powder instead of taco seasoning mix. Top burgers with sliced Canadian Mozzarella cheese and sautéed mushrooms.

Ham and Rice Florentine

¼ cup	butter	50 mL
½ cup	chopped onion	125 mL
1	garlic clove, minced	1
¼ cup	all-purpose flour	50 mL
1 tsp	chicken bouillon mix	5 mL
2½ cups	milk	625 mL
2 cups	shredded Canadian Cheddar cheese*	500 mL
1	pkg (300 g) frozen chopped spinach, thawed	1
	salt and pepper	
3 cups	cooked rice	750 mL
6	slices cooked ham	6
	shredded Canadian Cheddar cheese	

◄ Preheat oven to 350°F (180°C).

◄ In medium saucepan, melt butter. Sauté onion and garlic until tender. Blend in flour and bouillon mix. Gradually stir in milk. Cook and stir over medium heat until mixture boils and thickens. Remove from heat.

◄ Add Cheddar cheese and stir until cheese is melted. Drain spinach and squeeze dry; stir into melted cheese. Season with salt and pepper to taste.

◄ Spoon half of the rice into 2-qt (2-L) shallow rectangular casserole. Top with half the cheese sauce. Arrange ham slices over sauce. Layer remaining rice then cheese sauce over ham. Sprinkle with additional Cheddar cheese and bake 25 minutes or until heated through.

Makes 6 servings.
Preparation time: 25 minutes
Baking time: 25 minutes

* Or you can use shredded Canadian Swiss, Colby, Gouda *or* Mozzarella cheese.

Speedy Oven Meatballs

1 lb	lean ground beef	500 g
¼ cup	fine dry bread crumbs	50 mL
1	single-serving pkg mushroom soup mix	1
½ cup	milk	125 mL

◄ Preheat oven to 500°F (260°C).

◄ In large bowl, combine beef, bread crumbs, soup mix and milk; shape mixture into 32 balls. Place in single layer in large foil-lined shallow baking pan. Bake 8 minutes or until cooked; drain.

◄ Add meatballs to one of the following sauces and serve with hot cooked rice or noodles.

Makes 4 servings.
Preparation time: 10 minutes
Baking time: 8 minutes

Cheese Sauce: In medium saucepan, melt 2 tbsp (30 mL) butter. Blend in 2 tbsp (30 mL) flour and ¾ tsp (3 mL) dry mustard. Gradually stir in 1¼ cups (300 mL) milk. Cook and stir over medium heat until mixture boils and thickens. Remove from heat; cool slightly. Add 1½ cups (375 mL) shredded Canadian Cheddar cheese and stir until cheese is melted.

Makes about 1½ cups (375 mL).
Preparation time: 5 minutes
Cooking time: 10 minutes

Mushroom Sauce: In medium saucepan, combine 1 can (10 oz / 284 mL) cream of mushroom soup and ⅔ cup (150 mL) milk. Add 1 can (10 oz / 284 mL) drained, sliced mushrooms. Cook and stir over medium heat until hot.

Makes about 2½ cups (625 mL).
Preparation time: 5 minutes
Cooking time: 5 minutes

Curry Sauce: In medium saucepan, melt 2 tbsp (30 mL) butter. Blend in 2 tbsp (30 mL) flour, 1 tsp (5 mL) curry powder and pinch ground ginger. Gradually stir in ¾ cup (175 mL) light cream and ½ cup (125 mL) beef consommé. Cook and stir over medium heat until mixture boils and thickens.

Makes about 1½ cups (375 mL).
Preparation time: 5 minutes
Cooking time: 10 minutes

── TIP ──

To quickly shape uniform meatballs, place meat mixture on cutting board; pat evenly into large square, 1-inch (2.5-cm) thick. With sharp knife, cut meat into 32 squares; shape each square into a ball with wet hands.

Meatza Pie

1½ lbs	lean ground beef	750 g
1 cup	fine dry bread crumbs	250 mL
²/₃ cup	beef broth	150 mL
1	egg	1
½ cup	finely chopped onion	125 mL
½ tsp	garlic salt	2 mL
1	can (7½ oz / 213 mL) pizza sauce	1
2 cups	shredded Canadian Mozzarella cheese*	500 mL
	pizza toppings: sliced mushrooms, green peppers, olives, etc.	
2 tbsp	grated Canadian Parmesan cheese	30 mL

◄ Preheat oven to 350°F (180°C).

◄ In large bowl, combine beef, bread crumbs, broth, egg, onion and garlic salt; mix well. Press evenly into bottom of 12-inch (30-cm) pizza pan; form ½-inch (1-cm) rim around edge of pan. Spread pizza sauce over meat. Sprinkle Mozzarella cheese and pizza toppings over sauce. Sprinkle with Parmesan cheese.

◄ Bake 20 minutes or until meat is cooked. Cut into wedges and serve.

Makes one pizza.
Preparation time: 15 minutes
Baking time: 20 minutes

* Or you can use shredded Canadian Brick, Colby, Havarti *or* Provolone cheese.

Sausage and Bean Cassoulet

1½ lbs	Polish sausage	750 g
2	cans (14 oz/398 mL *each*) baked beans	2
2	cans (14 oz/398 mL *each*) red kidney beans, drained	2
1	can (14 oz/398 mL) lima beans, drained	1
3 cups	shredded Canadian Cheddar cheese*	750 mL
1	can (7½ oz/213 mL) tomato sauce	1
⅓ cup	molasses	75 mL
2 tsp	onion salt	10 mL
½ tsp	ground black pepper	2 mL
¼ tsp	dry mustard	1 mL

* Or you can use shredded Canadian Colby, Brick, Farmers' *or* Gouda cheese.

◄ Preheat oven to 350°F (180°C).

◄ Remove casing from sausage and cut into ½-inch (1-cm) thick slices. In 4-qt (4-L) baking dish or ovenproof mixing bowl, combine baked beans, kidney beans, lima beans, sausage and Cheddar cheese.

◄ In small bowl, combine tomato sauce, molasses, onion salt, pepper and dry mustard; pour over beans and stir to combine. Bake, uncovered, 1 hour. Stir and bake 15 minutes longer.

Makes 10 to 12 servings.
Preparation time: 10 minutes
Baking time: 1 hour and 15 minutes

Shepherd's Pie with Cheesy Mashed Potatoes

1½ lbs	lean ground beef	750 g
2 cups	sliced fresh mushrooms	500 mL
2	cans (7½ oz / 213 mL *each*) pizza sauce	2
1	pkg (about 43 g) spaghetti sauce mix	1
2 cups	frozen cut green beans	500 mL
6	medium potatoes, peeled, quartered	6
¾ cup	warm milk	175 mL
2 tbsp	butter	30 mL
1¼ cups	shredded Canadian Cheddar cheese*, divided	300 mL
	salt and pepper	

◄ Preheat oven to 350°F (180°C).

◄ In large frypan, combine beef and mushrooms. Sauté until beef is browned and mushrooms are tender. Drain. Stir in pizza sauce, spaghetti sauce mix and green beans. Spoon meat mixture into 2-qt (2-L) shallow rectangular baking dish.

◄ In large saucepan, cook potatoes in boiling salted water 20 minutes or until tender; drain. Mash with milk and butter. Stir in 1 cup (250 mL) of the Cheddar cheese. Add salt and pepper to taste.

◄ Spread mashed potatoes over meat and vegetable layer. Sprinkle remaining ¼ cup (50 mL) Cheddar cheese over top. Bake 30 minutes or until heated through.

Makes 6 servings.
Preparation time: 15 minutes
Baking time: 30 minutes

*Or you can use shredded Canadian Colby *or* Mozzarella cheese.

Easy Pork Goulash

2 tbsp	butter	30 mL
2	medium onions, thinly sliced	2
2 tsp	*each* paprika and chicken bouillon mix	10 mL
1½ tsp	garlic salt	7 mL
1¼ cups	water, divided	300 mL
2 lbs	lean boneless stewing pork, cut in 1-inch (2.5-cm) cubes	1 kg
3 tbsp	flour	45 mL
1 cup	plain yogourt	250 mL
1 tsp	sugar	5 mL
	hot cooked rice *or* noodles	

◄ In large saucepan or Dutch oven, melt butter. Sauté onions until tender. Blend in paprika, bouillon mix and garlic salt. Add 1 cup (250 mL) of the water and pork. Bring to a boil over medium-high heat. Reduce heat, cover and simmer 1½ hours or until meat is tender; stir occasionally.

◄ Gradually stir remaining ¼ cup (50 mL) water into flour until smooth; add to meat mixture. Cook and stir over medium heat until mixture boils and thickens.

◄ Combine yogourt and sugar; stir into meat mixture. Reheat to serving temperature, stirring constantly; do not boil. Serve over rice.

Makes 6 servings.
Preparation time: 20 minutes
Cooking time: 1 hour and 45 minutes

Freezer Cheddar Beef Sauce

4 lbs	lean ground beef	2 kg
1 cup	finely chopped onion	250 mL
3	cans (14 oz/398 mL *each*) tomato sauce	3
1 tbsp	*each* salt and Worcestershire sauce	15 mL
4 cups	shredded Canadian Cheddar cheese	1 L

◄ In large saucepan or Dutch oven, combine beef and onion. Sauté until beef is browned and onion is tender; drain.

◄ Add tomato sauce, salt and Worcestershire sauce to pan. Bring to a boil over medium-high heat. Reduce heat, cover and simmer 45 minutes; stir occasionally. Remove from heat. Add Cheddar cheese and stir until cheese is melted. Cool.

◄ Divide mixture into 4 equal parts and freeze in plastic containers or plastic zipper storage bags. Thaw and use as needed for Spaghetti Sauce, Chili con Carne or Lasagna (recipes follow).

Makes 12 cups (4 L).
Preparation time: 20 minutes
Cooking time: 50 minutes

Spaghetti Sauce

1	container Freezer Cheddar Beef Sauce, thawed	1
1	can (14 oz/398 mL) whole tomatoes	1
1	can (10 oz/284 mL) sliced mushrooms, drained	1
1	can (5½ oz/156 mL) tomato paste	1
1	garlic clove, minced	1
1	bay leaf	1

◄ In large saucepan, combine Freezer Cheddar Beef Sauce, tomatoes, mushrooms, tomato paste, garlic and bay leaf. Bring to a boil over medium-high heat. Reduce heat, cover and simmer 20 minutes, stirring occasionally. Remove bay leaf. Pour sauce over hot cooked spaghetti and serve.

Makes 4 servings.
Preparation time: 5 minutes
Cooking time: 20 minutes

Spaghetti Sauce

Chili con Carne

1	container Freezer Cheddar Beef Sauce, thawed	1
1	can (19 oz/540 mL) red kidney beans, drained	1
1	can (14 oz/398 mL) whole tomatoes	1
1 tbsp	chili powder	15 mL
	additional shredded Canadian Cheddar cheese	

◄ In large saucepan, combine Freezer Cheddar Beef Sauce, beans, tomatoes and chili powder. Bring to a boil over medium-high heat. Reduce heat; cover and simmer 30 minutes; stir occasionally.

◄ Sprinkle Cheddar cheese over each serving.

Makes 4 servings.
Preparation time: 5 minutes
Cooking time: 30 minutes

Lasagna

1	container Freezer Cheddar Beef Sauce, thawed	1
1	can (5½ oz / 156 mL) tomato paste	1
½ tsp	dried oregano	2 mL
8	lasagna noodles, cooked, drained	8
1 cup	Cottage cheese	250 mL
1	pkg (200 g) Canadian Mozzarella cheese slices	1
	grated Canadian Parmesan cheese	

◄ Preheat oven to 375°F (190°C).

◄ In large bowl, combine Freezer Cheddar Beef Sauce, tomato paste and oregano. Spread a thin layer of meat sauce over bottom of 2-qt (2-L) shallow rectangular baking dish.

◄ Layer half the noodles, half the remaining sauce, all the Cottage cheese and half the Mozzarella cheese. Repeat layers with remaining ingredients. Sprinkle with Parmesan cheese. Bake 35 minutes or until heated through.

Makes 6 servings.
Preparation time: 15 minutes
Baking time: 35 minutes

Meatloaf Milano

Meatloaf Milano

1 lb	lean ground beef	500 g
½ lb	lean ground pork	250 g
1	pkg (about 70 g) mushroom soup mix	1
½ cup	fine dry bread crumbs	125 mL
½ cup	finely chopped onion	125 mL
1	egg	1
1	can (7½ oz/213 mL) pizza sauce, divided	1
4 oz	Canadian Mozzarella cheese*, thinly sliced	125 g

◄ Preheat oven to 375°F (190°C).

◄ In large bowl, combine beef, pork, soup mix, bread crumbs, onion, egg and half of the pizza sauce; mix well. Press into 9-inch (23-cm) pie plate.

◄ Bake 40 minutes or until done. Drain. Spread remaining pizza sauce over meat; arrange Mozzarella cheese on top. Bake 5 minutes longer or until cheese is melted. Cut into wedges and serve.

Makes 6 servings.
Preparation time: 10 minutes
Baking time: 45 minutes

* Or you can use thinly sliced Canadian Provolone *or* Fontina cheese.

Meatloaf Canadiana

1½ lbs	lean ground beef	750 g
1	pkg (about 50 g) onion soup mix	1
½ cup	fine dry bread crumbs	125 mL
1	egg	1
½ cup	milk	125 mL
½ cup	bottled barbecue *or* chili sauce	125 mL
4 oz	Canadian Cheddar cheese*, thinly sliced	125 g

◄ Preheat oven to 375°F (190°C).

◄ In large bowl, combine beef, soup mix, bread crumbs, egg and milk. Press into 9-inch (23-cm) pie plate.

◄ Bake 40 minutes or until done. Drain. Spread barbecue sauce over meat; arrange Cheddar cheese on top. Bake 5 minutes longer or until cheese is melted. Cut into wedges and serve.

Makes 6 servings.
Preparation time: 10 minutes
Baking time: 45 minutes

* Or you can use thinly sliced Canadian Brick *or* Colby cheese.

BREADS, MUFFINS AND PANCAKES

Maple Walnut Bread
with Creamy Maple Butter

2½ cups	all-purpose flour	625 mL
1 cup	sugar	250 mL
1 tbsp	baking powder	15 mL
1 tsp	salt	5 mL
2	eggs	2
1¼ cups	milk	300 mL
⅓ cup	butter, melted	75 mL
1 tsp	maple extract	5 mL
1½ cups	coarsely chopped walnuts (toasted, if desired)	375 mL
	Creamy Maple Butter	

◄ Preheat oven to 350°F (180°C).

◄ In large bowl, stir together flour, sugar, baking powder and salt.

◄ In medium bowl, lightly beat eggs. Stir in milk, butter and maple extract. Add to dry ingredients, all at once, stirring just until moistened. Stir in walnuts. Pour batter into greased 9 x 5 x 3-inch (23 x 13 x 8-cm) loaf pan.

◄ Bake 1 hour or until toothpick inserted in centre comes out clean. Cool 10 minutes in pan on wire rack. Remove from pan and let cool completely. Slice and serve with Creamy Maple Butter.

Makes 1 loaf.
Preparation time: 15 minutes
Baking time: 1 hour

Creamy Maple Butter: Cream ½ cup (125 mL) softened butter; gradually beat in ½ cup (125 mL) maple syrup. *Makes about 1¼ cups (300 mL).*

— TIP —

Toasting nuts intensifies their flavour: Spread chopped walnuts evenly on baking sheet. Bake at 350°F (180°C) 6 minutes or until golden brown. Let cool completely.

Cherry Crumble Cakes

2¼ cups	all-purpose flour	550 mL
¾ cup	sugar	175 mL
¾ cup	firm butter	175 mL
½ tsp	*each* baking powder and baking soda	2 mL
½ cup	finely chopped nuts	125 mL
1	egg	1
1 cup	plain yogourt	250 mL
2 tsp	grated lemon *or* orange rind	10 mL
1	can (19 oz/540 mL) cherry pie filling*	1

◄ Preheat oven to 350°F (180°C).

◄ In large bowl, stir together flour and sugar. Cut in butter with pastry blender or two knives until mixture is crumbly; set aside ½ cup (125 mL) of the mixture. To remainder add baking powder, baking soda and nuts.

◄ In small bowl, lightly beat egg; stir in yogourt and lemon rind. Add to dry ingredients, all at once, stirring just until moistened.

◄ Spread two-thirds of batter over bottom and part way up sides of eight greased 1½-cup (300-mL) custard cups or 4½ x 1¼-inch (11 x 3-cm) foil tart pans. Spoon cherry pie filling over batter. Drop remaining batter by small spoonfuls over filling. Sprinkle with reserved crumb mixture and place cups on baking sheet.

◄ Bake 25 minutes or until toothpick inserted in centre comes out clean. Cool 10 minutes in cups on wire rack. Remove from cups and let cool completely.

* You can use blueberry, apple or raisin filling instead of cherry pie filling.

Makes 8 servings.
Preparation time: 15 minutes
Baking time: 25 minutes

Golden Penny Pancakes
with Sautéed Apple Wedges

¾ cup	all-purpose flour	175 mL
1½ tsp	*each* baking powder and sugar	7 mL
¼ tsp	salt	1 mL
1 cup	shredded Canadian Cheddar cheese*	250 mL
1	egg	1
1 cup	milk	250 mL
2 tbsp	butter, melted	30 mL
	sautéed apple wedges**	
	maple syrup	

◄ In medium bowl, combine flour, baking powder, sugar and salt. Stir in Cheddar cheese.

◄ In small bowl, lightly beat egg; stir in milk and butter. Add to dry ingredients, all at once, stirring just until moistened.

◄ For each pancake, spread 1 level tbsp (15 mL) batter in lightly-greased frypan or griddle over medium-high heat. Cook until bubbles appear on the surface; turn and brown underside. Serve with sautéed apple wedges and maple syrup.

** Peel apples if desired, cut into wedges and sauté in 1 tbsp (15 mL) of butter until tender.

Makes 6 servings.
Preparation time: 10 minutes
Cooking time: 20 minutes

* Or you can use shredded Canadian Colby cheese.

Cheddar Muffins with Apple Butter

2 cups	all-purpose flour	500 mL
½ cup	sugar	125 mL
1 tbsp	baking powder	15 mL
1 tsp	salt	5 mL
½ tsp	baking soda	2 mL
1½ cups	shredded Canadian Cheddar cheese*	375 mL
2	eggs	2
1 cup	plain yogourt	250 mL
¼ cup	butter, melted	50 mL
	Apple Butter	

* Or you can use shredded Canadian *Swiss or* Gouda cheese.

◄ Preheat oven to 400°F (200°C).

◄ In large bowl, combine flour, sugar, baking powder, salt and baking soda; stir in Cheddar cheese.

◄ In small bowl, lightly beat eggs; stir in yogourt and butter. Add to dry ingredients, all at once, stirring just until moistened. Divide batter evenly among 12 large greased muffin cups.

◄ Bake 18 minutes or until toothpick inserted in centre comes out clean. Cool 10 minutes in cups on wire rack. Remove from cups and let cool completely. Serve with Apple Butter.

Makes 1 dozen muffins.
Preparation time: 10 minutes
Baking time: 18 minutes

Apple Butter: Cream together ½ cup (125 mL) softened butter, ⅓ cup (75 mL) apple jelly and ¼ tsp (1 mL) ground cinnamon. *Makes about 1 cup (250 mL).*

—TIP—

You can freeze muffins for up to two months: Allow them to cool completely then wrap in foil or place in airtight container or plastic bags before freezing. To reheat, cover lightly with foil and place in 350°F (180°C) oven 10 to 15 minutes.

Combine flour, sugar, baking powder, salt and baking soda; stir in Cheddar cheese.

In small bowl, lightly beat eggs and stir in yogourt and butter.

Add to dry ingredients, all at once, stirring just until moistened.

Golden Cheddar Bread

2 cups	all-purpose flour	500 mL
4 tsp	baking powder	20 mL
1 tbsp	sugar	15 mL
1 tsp	dry mustard	5 mL
½ tsp	salt	2 mL
1½ cups	shredded 'old' Canadian Cheddar cheese*	375 mL
1	egg	1
1 cup	milk	250 mL
¼ cup	butter, melted	50 mL
	paprika	

* Or you can use shredded Canadian Colby *or* Swiss cheese.

◄ Preheat oven to 350°F (180°C).

◄ In large bowl, combine flour, baking powder, sugar, mustard and salt; stir in Cheddar cheese.

◄ In small bowl, lightly beat egg; stir in milk and butter. Add to dry ingredients, all at once, stirring just until moistened. Spread batter into greased 8½ x 4½-inch (21 x 11-cm) loaf pan. Sprinkle with paprika.

◄ Bake 40 minutes or until toothpick inserted in centre comes out clean. Cool 10 minutes in pan on wire rack. Remove from pan and let cool completely.

Makes 1 loaf.
Preparation time: 15 minutes
Baking time: 40 minutes

—TIP—

Stir batter only until dry ingredients are moistened. If overmixed, bread will be tough and uneven.

For each pancake, spread about 1/3 cup (75 mL) batter in lightly greased frypan or griddle over medium heat.

Cook until bubbles appear on the surface.

Turn and brown underside.

Maple Nut Pancakes
with Hot Buttery Maple Syrup

1½ cups	all-purpose flour	375 mL
¾ tsp	*each* baking powder, baking soda and salt	3 mL
¾ cup	chopped toasted walnuts *or* pecans	175 mL
2	eggs	2
¾ cup	plain yogourt	175 mL
¾ cup	milk	175 mL
¼ cup	butter, melted	50 mL
½ tsp	maple extract (optional)	2 mL
	Hot Buttery Maple Syrup	

◄ In large bowl, combine flour, baking powder, baking soda and salt; add walnuts.

◄ In small bowl, lightly beat eggs; stir in yogourt, milk, butter and maple extract, if desired. Add to dry ingredients, all at once, stirring until just moistened. Batter should be thick.

◄ For each pancake, spread about 1/3 cup (75 mL) batter in lightly greased frypan or griddle over medium heat. Cook until bubbles appear on the surface; turn and brown underside. Serve with Hot Buttery Maple Syrup.

Makes 4 servings.
Preparation time: 10 minutes
Cooking time: 20 minutes

Hot Buttery Maple Syrup: In small saucepan, combine 1 cup (250 mL) maple syrup and 1/2 cup (125 mL) butter. Cook and stir over medium heat until butter is melted. Let cool slightly and stir well before serving. *Makes 1 1/2 cups (375 mL).*

— TIP —

To make alphabet pancakes, omit nuts and fill empty ketchup or mustard squeeze bottles with batter. Cut nozzle to enlarge opening. Heat greased non-stick frypan over medium heat. For each pancake, squeeze batter from bottle into frypan to make different letters.

Parmesan Pick-Up Sticks

⅓ cup	grated Canadian Parmesan cheese	75 mL
1 tsp	poppy seeds	5 mL
3	hot dog buns	3
¼ cup	butter, melted	50 mL

◄ Preheat oven to 425°F (220°C).

◄ In small bowl, combine Parmesan cheese and poppy seeds. Cut each hot dog bun lengthwise into quarters and place on baking sheet. Brush cut sides with butter; sprinkle cheese mixture over wedges.

◄ Bake 5 minutes or until golden and crisp. Let cool on wire rack.

Makes 12 sticks.
Preparation time: 5 minutes
Baking time: 5 minutes

Banana Bran Muffins with Strawberry Butter

1²/₃ cups	all-purpose flour	400 mL
1 tsp	*each* baking powder and baking soda	5 mL
¹/₂ cup	firm butter	125 mL
²/₃ cup	bran	150 mL
¹/₂ cup	chopped nuts	125 mL
1	egg	1
²/₃ cup	mashed ripe banana	150 mL
¹/₂ cup	plain yogourt	125 mL
¹/₂ cup	packed brown sugar	125 mL
1 tbsp	molasses	15 mL
	Strawberry Butter	

◄ Preheat oven to 375°F (190°C).

◄ In large bowl, combine flour, baking powder and baking soda. Cut in butter with pastry blender or two knives until mixture is crumbly. Stir in bran and nuts.

◄ In medium bowl, lightly beat egg; stir in banana, yogourt, brown sugar and molasses. Add to dry ingredients, all at once, stirring just until moistened. Divide batter evenly among 12 medium greased muffin cups.

◄ Bake 20 minutes or until toothpick inserted in centre comes out clean. Cool 10 minutes in cups on wire racks. Remove from cups and let cool completely. Serve with Strawberry Butter.

Makes 1 dozen muffins.
Preparation time: 15 minutes
Baking time: 20 minutes

Strawberry Butter: Cream together ¹/₂ cup (125 mL) softened butter and ¹/₂ cup (125 mL) strawberry jam. *Makes about 1 cup (250 mL).*

─TIP─

Add a topping treat to your muffins before you bake them. Over batter in muffin cups, sprinkle quick-cooking rolled oats, cinnamon and sugar, sesame seeds or chopped nuts.

Cheddar Scones

2¼ cups	all-purpose flour	550 mL
4 tsp	baking powder	20 mL
1 tbsp	sugar	15 mL
1 tsp	salt	5 mL
½ cup	shortening	125 mL
1	egg, beaten	1
1 cup	milk	250 mL
1 cup	shredded Canadian Cheddar cheese, divided	250 mL
1	egg yolk, beaten	1
	poppy seeds	

◄ Preheat oven to 450°F (230°C).

◄ In large bowl, combine flour, baking powder, sugar and salt. Cut in shortening with pastry blender or two knives until mixture is crumbly. Stir in egg, milk and ¾ cup (175 mL) of the Cheddar cheese, stirring just until moistened.

◄ Turn out on a lightly floured board and knead gently about 20 times, adding more flour to dough if necessary.

◄ Place dough on ungreased baking sheet. Pat or roll out to 8-inch (20-cm) circle. Cut into 8 wedges but do not separate. Brush with egg yolk and sprinkle with poppy seeds.

◄ Bake 12 minutes or until golden. Remove from oven and sprinkle with remaining Cheddar cheese. Return to oven until cheese is melted.

Makes 8 servings.
Preparation time: 15 minutes
Baking time: 14 minutes

Cut shortening into dry ingredients with pastry blender or two knives until mixture is crumbly.

Stir in egg, milk and ¾ cup (175 mL) of the Cheddar cheese, stirring just until moistened.

Turn out on a lightly floured board and knead gently about 20 times.

Roll dough into 8-inch (20-cm) circle.

Cut into 8 wedges but do not separate.

Brush with egg yolk and sprinkle with poppy seeds.

DESSERTS, TARTS, CAKES AND PIES

Sour Cream Apple Pie

¾ cup	packed brown sugar, divided	175 mL
1½ tbsp	flour	25 mL
¼ tsp	salt	1 mL
1	egg	1
1 cup	sour cream	250 mL
1½ tsp	vanilla	7 mL
3 cups	sliced peeled apples	750 mL
1	9-inch (23-cm) pie shell*, unbaked	1
¼ cup	all-purpose flour	50 mL
½ tsp	ground cinnamon	2 mL
2 tbsp	firm butter	30 mL

◄ Preheat oven to 400°F (200°C).

◄ In large bowl, combine ½ cup (125 mL) of the brown sugar, 1½ tbsp (25 mL) flour and salt. Add egg and mix well. Stir in sour cream and vanilla. Add apples and toss lightly. Turn into prepared pie shell and bake 10 minutes.

◄ In medium bowl, combine ¼ cup (50 mL) flour, remaining ¼ cup (50 mL) brown sugar and cinnamon; cut in butter with pastry blender or two knives until crumbly. Sprinkle evenly over pie.

◄ Reduce oven temperature to 350°F (180°C) and bake 40 minutes or until set. Cool on wire rack.

* If you are using a frozen 9-inch (23-cm) deep dish pie shell, place on baking sheet and thaw 10 minutes before filling with batter.

Makes 8 servings.
Preparation time: 20 minutes
Baking time: 50 minutes

Best-Ever Butter Tarts

	pastry for double crust 9-inch (23-cm) pie*	
1 cup	raisins (optional)	250 mL
3	eggs	3
1 cup	corn syrup	250 mL
2/3 cup	packed brown sugar	150 mL
1/3 cup	butter, melted	75 mL
	pinch salt	

◄ Preheat oven to 375°F (190°C).

◄ Roll out pastry and cut into twelve 5-inch (13-cm) circles. Set each circle loosely into 3-inch (7.5-cm) muffin cup. Sprinkle raisins over bottom of each tart shell, if desired, and chill.

◄ In medium bowl, combine eggs, corn syrup, brown sugar, butter and salt. Pour over raisins.

◄ Bake 20 minutes or until set. Cool 5 minutes in pans on wire racks. Remove from pans and let cool completely.

* Or you can use 2 dozen 3-inch (7.5-cm) frozen tart shells, placed on baking sheets and thawed 10 minutes.

Makes 1 dozen large tarts.
Preparation time: 20 minutes
Baking time: 20 minutes

Maple Syrup Tarts

⅓ cup	butter	75 mL
⅓ cup	all-purpose flour	75 mL
½ cup	water	125 mL
1½ cups	maple syrup	375 mL
24	3-inch (7.5-cm) frozen tart shells, baked, cooled	24

◄ In medium saucepan, melt butter. Blend in flour. Gradually stir in water, then maple syrup. Cook and stir over medium heat until mixture boils and thickens. Let cool a few minutes.

◄ Pour into tart shells and let stand until cooled and set.

Makes 2 dozen tarts.
Preparation time: 5 minutes
Cooking time: 5 minutes
Cooling time: 2 hours

Old-Fashioned Cheesecake

1½ cups	graham cracker crumbs	375 mL
¼ cup	butter, melted	50 mL
3	pkgs (250 g *each*)· Cream cheese, softened	3
1 cup	sugar	250 mL
3	eggs	3
1 tsp	vanilla	5 mL
1½ cups	sour cream, divided	375 mL
3 tbsp	sugar	45 mL
1 tsp	vanilla	5 mL
	fresh fruit	

◄ Preheat oven to 350°F (180°C).

◄ In small bowl, combine cracker crumbs and butter. Press onto bottom of 9-inch (23-cm) springform pan.

◄ In large mixer bowl, beat Cream cheese until light and fluffy; gradually beat in 1 cup (250 mL) sugar. Add eggs, one at a time, beating well after each addition. Stir in vanilla and ½ cup (125 mL) of the sour cream. Pour over prepared crust.

◄ Bake 45 minutes or until just set when gently shaken.

◄ In small bowl, combine remaining 1 cup (250 mL) sour cream, 3 tbsp (45 mL) sugar and vanilla. Spread over hot cheesecake. Bake 5 minutes longer. Remove from oven and let cool on wire rack. Chill well before serving with fresh fruit.

Makes 8 to 10 servings.
Preparation time: 15 minutes
Baking time: 50 minutes

—TIP—

To serve cheesecake, dip knife into very hot water and wipe dry before slicing. To soften Cream cheese quickly, remove the wrapper and microwave on HIGH (100%) 15 seconds.

1

In small bowl, combine cracker crumbs and butter.

2

Beat Cream cheese until light and fluffy; gradually beat in sugar. Add eggs, one at a time, beating well after each addition.

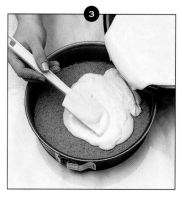

3

Stir in vanilla and sour cream and pour over prepared crust.

Vanilla Cream

1 cup	cold whipping cream	250 mL
1	pkg (125 g) Cream cheese, softened	1
2/3 cup	icing sugar	150 mL
2 tsp	vanilla	10 mL

◄ In small mixer bowl, whip cream until stiff.

◄ In another small mixer bowl, with same beaters, beat Cream cheese until smooth; gradually beat in sugar and vanilla. Stir a small amount of whipped cream into Cream cheese mixture; fold in remaining whipped cream. Spoon over berries, plain cake or fruit salad.

Makes about 2½ cups (625 mL).
Preparation time: 10 minutes

Banana Maple Cream

1 cup	cold whipping cream	250 mL
1	pkg (125 g) Cream cheese, softened	1
1/3 cup	maple syrup	75 mL
1/2 cup	mashed ripe banana	125 mL

◄ In small mixer bowl, whip cream until stiff.

◄ In another small mixer bowl, with same beaters, beat Cream cheese until smooth; gradually beat in maple syrup and banana. Fold in whipped cream. Spoon over berries, plain cake or fruit salad.

Makes about 3 cups (750 mL).
Preparation time: 10 minutes

Honey Yogourt Cream

1	pkg (125 g) Cream cheese, softened	1
3 tbsp	liquid honey	45 mL
1 cup	vanilla yogourt	250 mL
1/4-1/2 tsp	grated lemon rind	1-2 mL

◄ In small mixer bowl, beat Cream cheese until smooth; gradually beat in honey. Stir in yogourt and lemon rind. Spoon over berries, plain cake or fruit salad.

Makes about 2²/₃ cups (650 mL).
Preparation time: 10 minutes

Strawberry Lemonade Tarts

3	eggs	3
²/₃ cup	sugar	150 mL
1 tbsp	grated lemon rind	15 mL
½ cup	lemon juice	125 mL
1 cup	cold whipping cream	250 mL
24	3-inch (7.5-cm) tart shells, baked, cooled	24
	fresh mint leaves	
	fresh strawberries	

◄ In small mixer bowl, lightly beat eggs. Beat in sugar until thick and light. Stir in lemon rind and juice. Place mixture in medium saucepan. Cook and stir over low heat until smooth and thick. Remove from heat. Cover surface directly with plastic wrap and let cool completely.

◄ In small mixer bowl, whip cream until stiff. Fold into cooled lemon mixture and chill well. Just before serving, spoon filling into prepared tart shells and top each tart with mint leaves and a fresh strawberry.

Makes 2 dozen tarts.
Preparation time: 20 minutes
Cooking time: 10 minutes
Chilling time: 2 hours

— TIP —

Whipping cream doubles in volume when it's whipped. To get 2 cups (500 mL) whipped cream start with 1 cup (250 mL) whipping cream. For best results, chill the bowl and beaters before whipping cold cream.

Silky Chocolate Sauce

1	pkg (175 g) semi-sweet chocolate chips	1
1/3 cup	corn syrup	75 mL
3/4 cup	whipping cream	175 mL

◄ In medium saucepan, combine chocolate chips and corn syrup. Cook and stir over low heat until smooth. Gradually stir in whipping cream. Continue cooking and stirring until hot. Serve warm or cool over ice cream.

Makes about 1²/₃ cups (400 mL).
Preparation time: 5 minutes
Cooking time: 5 minutes

Classic Butterscotch Sauce

1/3 cup	butter	75 mL
1 cup	packed brown sugar	250 mL
2/3 cup	whipping cream	150 mL
2 tbsp	corn syrup	30 mL

◄ In medium saucepan, melt butter. Stir in sugar, whipping cream and corn syrup. Bring mixture to a boil over low heat, stirring constantly. Serve warm or cool over ice cream.

Makes about 1½ cups (375 mL).
Preparation time: 5 minutes
Cooking time: 5 minutes

Buttery Maple Walnut Sauce

1 cup	maple syrup	250 mL
2 tbsp	butter	30 mL
1/4 cup	whipping cream	50 mL
1/4 cup	chopped toasted walnuts	50 mL

◄ In medium saucepan, combine maple syrup and butter. Over medium heat, bring mixture to a boil and boil 3 minutes, stirring constantly. Let cool. Stir in whipping cream and nuts. Serve warm or cool over ice cream.

Makes about 1¼ cups (300 mL).
Preparation time: 5 minutes
Cooking time: 5 minutes

Buttery Maple Walnut Sauce (top), Silky Chocolate Sauce, Classic Butterscotch Sauce

1

Combine apples, cider, brown sugar and butter. Bring mixture to a boil over medium heat, stirring constantly.

2

In small bowl, combine water, corn starch and cinnamon; stir into apple mixture.

3

In large bowl, combine biscuit baking mix, Cheddar cheese and granulated sugar.

Apple 'n' Cider Cobbler

8 cups	cubed, peeled apples	2 L
1½ cups	apple cider *or* juice	375 mL
½ cup	packed brown sugar	125 mL
3 tbsp	butter	45 mL
2 tbsp	*each* water and corn starch	30 mL
1 tsp	ground cinnamon	5 mL
2 cups	biscuit baking mix	500 mL
1 cup	shredded Canadian Cheddar cheese*	250 mL
2 tbsp	granulated sugar	30 mL
½ cup	milk	125 mL
	light *or* table cream (optional)	

* Or you can use shredded Canadian Colby *or* Gouda cheese.

◄ In large saucepan, combine apples, cider, brown sugar and butter. Bring mixture to a boil over medium heat, stirring constantly. Reduce heat, cover and simmer 10 minutes or until apples are tender.

◄ Preheat oven to 400°F (200°C).

◄ In small bowl, combine water, corn starch and cinnamon; stir into apple mixture. Cook and stir over medium heat until mixture boils and thickens. Cover and keep warm.

◄ In large bowl, combine biscuit baking mix, Cheddar cheese and granulated sugar. Add milk and mix lightly with fork.

◄ Return apple mixture to a boil and pour into 4-qt (4-L) casserole or ovenproof mixing bowl. Drop spoonfuls of batter over hot fruit.

◄ Bake 20 minutes or until golden brown and bubbly. Serve warm with light cream, if desired.

Makes 8 servings.
Preparation time: 30 minutes
Baking time: 20 minutes

Add milk and mix lightly with fork.

Return apple mixture to a boil and pour into 4-qt (4-L) casserole or ovenproof mixing bowl.

Drop spoonfuls of batter over hot fruit.

COOKIES
AND SQUARES

Raisin Oatmeal Cookies

1 cup + 2 tbsp	all-purpose flour	250 mL + 30 mL
1 tsp	baking powder	5 mL
½ tsp	salt	2 mL
	pinch baking soda	
½ cup	butter, softened	125 mL
¾ cup	packed brown sugar	175 mL
½ cup	mashed ripe banana	125 mL
1	egg	1
1 tsp	vanilla	5 mL
1 cup	quick-cooking rolled oats	250 mL
1¼ cups	raisins	300 mL

◄ Preheat oven to 375°F (190°C).

◄ In medium bowl, combine flour, baking powder, salt and baking soda.

◄ In large mixer bowl, cream butter until light and fluffy; gradually beat in sugar. Beat in banana, egg and vanilla. Stir in dry ingredients, rolled oats and raisins.

◄ Drop tablespoons (15 mL) of batter, one dozen at a time, onto greased baking sheets. Spread cookies into 2-inch (5-cm) circles.

◄ Bake 10 minutes or until lightly browned around edges. Remove from baking sheets and let cool on wire racks.

Makes about 3 dozen cookies.
Preparation time: 15 minutes
Baking time: 10 minutes

Variation: For a change of pace, you can use dried apricots, cherries *or* cranberries, trail mix *or* chopped dates instead of raisins.

Harvest Butternut Squares

1 cup	all-purpose flour	250 mL
¼ cup	granulated sugar	50 mL
½ cup	firm butter	125 mL
2	eggs	2
1½ cups	packed brown sugar	375 mL
¼ cup	butter, melted	50 mL
1 tbsp	vinegar	15 mL
1 tsp	vanilla	5 mL
⅔ cup	coarsely chopped walnuts	150 mL
½ cup	golden raisins	125 mL
	walnut halves (optional)	

◄ Preheat oven to 350°F (180°C).

◄ In medium bowl, combine flour and granulated sugar. Cut in ½ cup (125 mL) butter with pastry blender or two knives until mixture is crumbly. Press onto bottom of ungreased 9-inch (23-cm) square baking pan. Bake 10 minutes.

◄ In medium bowl, lightly beat eggs. Beat in brown sugar, ¼ cup (50 mL) butter, vinegar and vanilla. Stir in nuts and raisins. Pour over hot crust.

◄ Bake 30 minutes longer or until set. Let cool in pan on wire rack. Cut into squares and garnish with walnut halves, if desired.

Makes 9 large or 36 small squares.
Preparation time: 15 minutes
Baking time: 40 minutes

—TIP—

Place the oven rack in centre of the oven for even browning.

Yummy Yogourt Pops

1 cup	plain yogourt	250 mL
³/₄ cup	frozen orange juice concentrate	175 mL
³/₄ cup	cold milk	175 mL

◄ In blender container, combine yogourt, juice concentrate and milk. Cover and blend at high speed until smooth.

◄ Pour into 12 popsicle molds *or* 6 small paper cups. Freeze until partially firm, then insert wooden stick into each pop. Freeze until firm.

Makes 12 pops
Preparation time: 5 minutes
Freezing time: 6 to 12 hours

— TIP —

You can use any flavour of frozen juice concentrate in this recipe.

177 ~

Cheddar Date Bars

1½ cups	all-purpose flour	375 mL
2 tsp	baking powder	10 mL
½ tsp	salt	2 mL
½ cup	butter	125 mL
1½ cups	packed brown sugar	375 mL
2	eggs	2
2 tsp	vanilla	10 mL
1½ cups	shredded Canadian Cheddar cheese	375 mL
1 cup	*each* chopped dates and walnuts	250 mL

◄ Preheat oven to 350°F (180°C).

◄ In medium bowl, combine flour, baking powder and salt.

◄ In large saucepan, melt butter. Remove from heat and stir in sugar. Beat in eggs and vanilla.

◄ Stir in dry ingredients, Cheddar cheese, dates and walnuts. Spread batter in greased 13 x 9 x 2-inch (33 x 23 x 5-cm) baking pan.

◄ Bake 30 minutes or until golden brown. Let cool in pan on wire rack. Cut into bars.

Makes 9 large or 36 small bars.
Preparation time: 20 minutes
Baking time: 30 minutes

— TIP —

For a festive look, cut bars into diamonds or triangles.

Crispy Chocolate Peanut Squares

½ cup	butter	125 mL
½ cup	unsweetened cocoa powder	125 mL
1 cup	peanut butter	250 mL
¾ cup	liquid honey	175 mL
¼ cup	granulated sugar	50 mL
3 cups	crisp rice cereal	750 mL
2 cups	peanuts, chopped	500 mL
1 tsp	vanilla	5 mL

◄ In large saucepan, melt butter; stir in cocoa. Add peanut butter, honey and sugar. Cook and stir over medium heat until hot and smooth. Remove from heat.

◄ Add cereal, nuts and vanilla; stir until well-combined. Press lightly into ungreased 9-inch (23-cm) square baking pan.

◄ Chill 2 hours or until set. Cut into squares. Store covered in refrigerator.

Makes 15 large or 36 small squares.
Preparation time: 20 minutes
Chilling time: 2 hours

Luscious Lemon Bars

1⅓ cups	all-purpose flour	325 mL
1 cup	granulated sugar, divided	250 mL
½ cup	butter, softened	125 mL
2	eggs	2
2 tbsp	all-purpose flour	30 mL
¼ tsp	baking powder	1 mL
1½ tsp	grated lemon rind	7 mL
3 tbsp	lemon juice	45 mL
	icing sugar	

◄ Preheat oven to 350°F (180°C).

◄ In small mixer bowl, beat together 1⅓ cups (325 mL) flour, ¼ cup (50 mL) of the sugar and butter until mixture is crumbly.

◄ Press onto bottom of ungreased 8-inch (20-cm) square baking pan. Bake 15 minutes or until edges are lightly browned.

◄ In small mixer bowl, beat together remaining granulated sugar, eggs, 2 tbsp (30 mL) flour, baking powder, lemon rind and juice. Pour filling over hot crust.

◄ Bake 15 minutes longer or until set. Let cool in pan on wire rack. Sprinkle with icing sugar and cut into bars.

Makes 15 large or 24 small bars.
Preparation time: 15 minutes
Baking time: 30 minutes

1

In small mixer bowl, beat together flour, ¼ cup (50 mL) sugar and butter until mixture is crumbly.

2

In small mixer bowl, beat together remaining sugar and flour, eggs, baking powder, lemon rind and juice.

3

Pour filling over hot crust.

Cheddar Granola Cookies

¾ cup	all-purpose flour	175 mL
½ cup	whole wheat flour	125 mL
1 tsp	*each* baking soda and salt	5 mL
½ cup	butter, softened	125 mL
½ cup	granulated sugar	125 mL
⅓ cup	liquid honey	75 mL
2	eggs	2
2 cups	granola	500 mL
2 cups	shredded Canadian Cheddar cheese	500 mL
1½ cups	golden raisins	375 mL

◄ Preheat oven to 350°F (180°C).

◄ In medium bowl, stir together all-purpose flour, whole wheat flour, baking soda and salt.

◄ In large mixer bowl, cream butter until light and fluffy; gradually beat in sugar and honey. Add eggs, one at a time, beating well after each addition.

◄ Stir in dry ingredients, granola, Cheddar cheese and raisins; mix well (batter should be stiff). Drop tablespoons (15 mL) of batter, 1 dozen at a time, about 2 inches (5 cm) apart, onto ungreased baking sheets. With floured fingers, pat into 2-inch (5-cm) circles.

◄ Bake 10 minutes or until lightly browned. Remove from baking sheets immediately; let cool on wire racks.

Makes about 5 dozen cookies.
Preparation time: 15 minutes
Baking time: 10 minutes

— TIP —

To store, place soft cookies in a container with a tight fitting lid; place crisp cookies in a container with a loose fitting lid. Do not store soft and crisp cookies together.

Double Chocolate Fudgey Brownies

1¼ cups	all-purpose flour	300 mL
1 tsp	baking powder	5 mL
1 cup	butter	250 mL
1 cup	unsweetened cocoa powder	250 mL
2 cups	granulated sugar	500 mL
4	eggs	4
1 tsp	vanilla	5 mL
1 cup	chopped walnuts	250 mL
1 cup	miniature chocolate chips	250 mL

◄ Preheat oven to 350°F (180°C).

◄ In medium bowl, combine flour and baking powder.

◄ In large saucepan, melt butter. Remove from heat and stir in cocoa. Blend in sugar, eggs and vanilla. Stir in dry ingredients.

◄ Spread batter in greased 13 x 9 x 2-inch (33 x 23 x 5-cm) baking pan. Sprinkle nuts and chocolate chips over batter; press down lightly.

◄ Bake 30 minutes or until toothpick inserted in centre comes out clean. Let cool in pan on wire rack. Cut into squares.

Makes 10 large or 30 small brownies.
Preparation time: 15 minutes
Baking time: 30 minutes

—TIP—

Overbaking brownies will make them dry. Closely follow the recommended baking times given in these recipes.

Mini Chip Butter Crisps

2¼ cups	all-purpose flour	550 mL
½ tsp	salt	2 mL
1¼ cups	butter, softened	300 mL
1 cup	icing sugar	250 mL
2 tsp	vanilla	10 mL
1½ cups	miniature chocolate chips	375 mL

◄ Preheat oven to 325°F (160°C).

◄ In medium bowl, combine flour and salt.

◄ In large mixer bowl, cream butter until light and fluffy; gradually beat in sugar and vanilla. Gradually add dry ingredients and blend until smooth. Stir in chocolate chips.

◄ Shape dough into 1-inch (2.5-cm) balls. Place, 1 dozen at a time, on ungreased baking sheets. Flatten to circles about 2 inches (5 cm) in diameter with bottom of glass dipped in flour.

◄ Bake 10 minutes or until done. Remove from baking sheets and let cool on wire racks.

Makes about 6 dozen cookies.
Preparation time: 20 minutes
Baking time: 10 minutes

— TIP —

Cookies may be wrapped well and frozen for up to 2 months.

In large mixer bowl, cream butter and peanut butter until light and fluffy; gradually beat in sugar, salt and vanilla.

Stir in dry ingredients, chocolate chips, coconut and peanuts.

Press mixture evenly into ungreased shallow baking pan.

Peanut Butter Cookie Brittle

1¼ cups	quick-cooking rolled oats	300 mL
1 cup	all-purpose flour	250 mL
½ cup	butter, softened	125 mL
½ cup	peanut butter	125 mL
¾ cup	packed brown sugar	175 mL
1 tsp	*each* salt and vanilla	5 mL
1	pkg (300 g) semi-sweet chocolate chips	1
½ cup	flaked coconut	125 mL
1 cup	chopped peanuts	250 mL

◄ Preheat oven to 375°F (190°C).

◄ In medium bowl, combine rolled oats and flour.

◄ In large mixer bowl, cream butter and peanut butter until light and fluffy; gradually beat in sugar, salt and vanilla. Stir in dry ingredients, chocolate chips, coconut and peanuts.

◄ Press mixture evenly into ungreased 15 x 10-inch (38 x 25-cm) shallow baking pan. Bake 20 minutes. Let cool in pan on wire rack. Break into irregular pieces.

Makes about 4 dozen pieces.
Preparation time: 15 minutes
Baking time: 20 minutes

—TIP—

For an extra peanut butter hit, you can use peanut butter chips instead of semi-sweet chocolate chips.

Chocolate Chocolate Chip Cookies

2¼ cups	all-purpose flour	550 mL
1½ tsp	baking soda	7 mL
½ cup	butter, softened	125 mL
1	pkg (250 g) Cream cheese, softened	1
1⅓ cups	granulated sugar	325 mL
1	egg	1
1	pkg (300 g) miniature chocolate chips, divided	1
⅓ cup	chopped nuts (optional)	75 mL

◀ Preheat oven to 350°F (180°C).

◀ In medium bowl, stir together flour and baking soda.

◀ In large mixer bowl, cream butter and Cream cheese until light and fluffy; gradually beat in sugar and egg.

◀ Melt 1 cup (250 mL) of the chocolate chips. Stir into batter. Stir in dry ingredients, remaining chocolate chips and nuts, if desired.

◀ Drop tablespoons (15 mL) of batter, one dozen at a time, onto ungreased baking sheets. Bake 10 minutes or until firm around edges. Remove from baking sheets and let cool on wire racks.

Makes about 4 dozen cookies.
Preparation time: 15 minutes
Baking time: 10 minutes

—TIP—

Check cookies after the minimum baking time given, and frequently afterwards until they are baked as desired.

Index